21 世纪全国高职高专财经管理类规划教材

会计英语基础教程
Accounting English

吴 冰 *主编*

任丽萍 赵蕊芬 *副主编*

张立俊 *主审*

内容简介

本书是"以内容为基础的"(content-based)会计专业英语教材。通过学习可以快速掌握会计通用词汇,提高语言技能;同时,可以快速掌握西方财务会计基本知识和流程,以提高会计专业素养。

本着提高专业英语水平的同时熟悉会计流程的宗旨,本书内容包括:会计概况(The Fundamental Concepts and Principles)、借方和贷方——复式记账法(Debits and Credits: The Double-Entry System)、记账和过账(Journalizing and Posting Transactions)、财务报表(Financial Statements)、调账和结账(Adjusting and Closing Procedures)和理财意识(Financial Awareness)等;最后提供了中华人民共和国会计法(Accounting Law of the People's Republic of China)、企业会计准则——基本准则(Accounting Standard for Business Enterprises: Basic Standard)、专业词汇总表(Glossary)和练习参考答案。

本书适合高职高专会计专业学生使用,也适合对会计英语感兴趣的读者作为参考资料。

图书在版编目(CIP)数据

会计英语基础教程/吴冰主编. —北京:北京大学出版社,2005.7
(21世纪全国高职高专财经管理类规划教材)
ISBN 978-7-301-09160-9

Ⅰ.会… Ⅱ.吴… Ⅲ.会计-英语-高等学校:技术学校-教材 Ⅳ.H31

中国版本图书馆 CIP 数据核字(2005)第 069425 号

书　　　名:	会计英语基础教程
著作责任者:	吴冰　主编
责 任 编 辑:	胡伟晔　刘标
标 准 书 号:	ISBN 978-7-301-09160-9/H·1496
出 　版　 者:	北京大学出版社
地　　　址:	北京市海淀区成府路205号　100871
电　　　话:	邮购部 62752015　发行部 62750672　编辑部 62765126　出版部 62754962
网　　　址:	http://www.pup.cn
电 子 信 箱:	xxjs@pup.pku.edu.cn
印　刷　者:	三河市博文印刷有限公司
发　行　者:	北京大学出版社
经　销　者:	新华书店

787 毫米×1092 毫米　16 开本　14.75 印张　323 千字
2005 年 7 月第 1 版　2017 年 5 月第 8 次印刷

定　　　价:32.00 元

未经许可,不得以任何方式复制或抄袭本书之部分或全部内容。
版权所有,侵权必究
举报电话:010-62752024;电子邮箱:fd@pup.pku.edu.cn

前　言

　　2001 年，教育部对大学的双语教学提出明确要求：力争在 3 年内，外语教学课程达到 5%～10%，暂不具备用外语授课条件的学校、专业可以对部分课程先实行外语教材、中文授课，分部到位。2004 年教育部在浙江大学召开了全国高校双语教学研讨会，决定每年在各个高校设立 100 门课程为双语教学，并规定双语课程要向经贸类专业倾斜。

　　我们说，在大学中有选择地推行双语教学既有其现实意义，也有需要克服的问题。第一，对于英语程度较高的学生，用国外原版专业教材，用英语授课，能使我们的学生在专业方面处于该领域的世界发展前沿。第二，并非所有课程、所有学生都适合双语教学。对于英语程度较低的学生，我们认为与其提出过高的、不切实际的大学双语教学要求，还不如扎扎实实地做好专业英语（ESP）教学的设计与实施工作，为学生真正打好外语应用能力的基础。结合专业知识的教学，目的在于提高学生英语学习的兴趣，提高学生英语使用能力的同时获得系统的学科专业知识。英语本来就是一种工具，只有通过英语这一工具广泛学习各个学科的知识，并在实际运用中使用，才能真正发展英语的能力。

　　本着这样的宗旨，本教材立足于会计专业英语和会计基础知识双语教学两方面兼顾；两年制和三年制的高职高专学生兼顾。整个编排注意了会计基础体系的顺序和完整性。传统的外语教材的内容主要包括课文、注释、语法规则和练习。而本书恰恰是"以内容为基础的"（content-based）会计专业英语教材，通过学习可以快速掌握会计通用语汇，提高语言技能；同时，可以快速掌握西方财务会计基本知识，以提高会计专业素养。

　　每一章节的内容我们做如下安排：

1. Section I　Accounting Study（会计学习）

　　先以每一章节的标题为中心，介绍西方财务会计基础知识和流程，并且用单词注解和术语注释的形式解释该章节的语言重点、专业难点。

2. Section II　Review & Exercises（复习与练习）

　　内容分为：
- Summary（小结）。以单词填空的形式归纳每一章的专业重点。
- Questions（简答）。以问题形式就语言、专业问题进行提问。
- Solved problems（会计业务练习）。用实际的会计业务题目来巩固专业知识，熟悉英语表达方式。

3. Section III　Reading Material（阅读材料）

　　会计英语课程应以在提高专业英语水平的同时熟悉会计流程为目标，运用词汇讲解、课文讲解、专业话题解释论述、复习与练习等多种多样的方法来提高课堂教学效果，活跃课堂教学气氛。

应该指出的是，作为本教程的特色——"复习与练习"是教材的重要组成部分，它不应当仅仅作为学生的课外作业。学生要学好这门实践性较强的课程，必须学会用英语来做实际的会计业务题，所以在课堂教学中应给予足够的重视。我们建议，每一章节都要利用一定的课堂教学时间进行复习与练习。文中标有※的为选学内容。

本教材的编写，先由主编拟订大纲，会同编著者讨论、修改。各章节具体分工如下：

吴冰，Chapter 6 和附录 4；

顾秀梅，Chapter 1、2；

王红蕾，Chapter 4；

陈彩珍，Chapter 3；

徐鲭，Chapter 5 和附录 1～附录 3。

最后由主编、副主编修改定稿。

一本书的成功，除了作者的劳动之外，更凝聚了许多人的支持和帮助，我对他们的贡献感激不尽。苏州经贸职业技术学院教务处领导张立俊和山西旅游职业学院任丽萍、赵蕊芬等对本教材的编写给予了热情关注和大力支持；感谢徐鲭老师提出了许多极有价值的修改意见。感谢北京大学出版社胡伟晔编辑为本书做了出色的编辑工作；还要感谢苏州经贸职业技术学院 03 会计班的同学，他们协助了部分文字的输入工作。在此谨向他们致以衷心的谢意。

由于时间仓促，水平有限，错误和不足在所难免，敬请广大读者指正。

编　者
2005 年 6 月

目 录

Chapter 1　The Fundamental Accounting Concepts and Principles（会计概述）............ 1
　Section I　Accounting Study（会计学习）... 1
　　1.1　Introduction（引言）... 1
　　1.2　The Accounting Profession（会计职业）.. 6
　　1.3　Accounting as an Information System（会计信息系统）............................. 11
　　※1.4　Accounting Principles and Concepts（会计原则和概念）....................... 15
　　1.5　Basic Elements of Financial Position: The Accounting Equation
　　　　（会计基本要素：会计等式）... 21
　Section II　Review & Exercises（复习与练习）... 29
　　　Summary 29
　　　Questions 30
　　　Solved Problems.. 30
　Section III　Reading Material（阅读材料）... 37
　　　The Assets Section of Balance Sheet... 37

Chapter 2　Debits and Credits: The Double-Entry System（借方和贷方：复式记账法）............ 39
　Section I　Accounting Study（会计学习）... 39
　　2.1　The Account（账户）.. 39
　　2.2　The Rules of Debit and Credit（借贷记账规则）....................................... 42
　　2.3　The Ledger and the Chart of Account（会计分类账与会计科目表）....... 49
　　2.4　The Trial Balance（试算平衡表）.. 52
　Section II　Review & Exercises（复习与练习）... 55
　　　Summary 55
　　　Questions 55
　　　Solved Problems.. 56
　Section III　Reading Material（阅读材料）... 62
　　　Discovery of Errors.. 62

Chapter 3　Journalizing and Posting Transactions（记账和过账）............................... 65
　Section I　Accounting Study（会计学习）... 65
　　3.1　The Journal（日记账）.. 65
　　3.2　Journalizing（登记日记账）... 70
　　3.3　Posting（过账）... 73

- Section II Review & Exercises（复习与练习） 76
  - Summary 76
  - Questions 76
  - Solved Problems 76
- Section III Reading Material（阅读材料） 86
  - Steps in the Accounting Cycle 86

Chapter 4 Financial Statements（财务报表） 89
- Section I Accounting Study（会计学习） 89
  - 4.1 Income Statement（损益表） 89
  - 4.2 Balance Sheet（资产负债表） 92
  - 4.3 Capital Statement（资本变动表） 94
  - 4.4 Financial Statement Summary（财务报表概述） 95
  - 4.5 Classified Financial Statements（分类财务报表） 96
- Section II Review & Exercises（复习与练习） 101
  - Summary 101
  - Questions 102
  - Solved problems 102
- Section III Reading Material（阅读材料） 106
  - Notes to the Financial Statements 106

Chapter 5 Adjusting and Closing Procedures（调账和结账） 108
- Section I Accounting Study（会计学习） 108
  - 5.1 Adjust Entries Covering Recorded Data（对已入账（会计）记录的调整分录） 108
  - 5.2 Adjusting Entries Covering Unrecorded Data（对未入账的（会计）记录的调整分录） 114
  - 5.3 Closing Entries（结账分录） 116
  - 5.4 Ruling Accounts（账户的划线结清） 120
  - 5.5 Post-Closing Trial Balance（结账后试算平衡表） 122
- Section II Review & Exercises（复习与练习） 123
  - Summary 123
  - Questions 124
  - Solved Problems 124
- Section III Reading Material（阅读材料） 132
  - Accrual Basis Accounting and Cash Basis Accounting 132

Chapter 6 Review: Financial Awareness（复习：财务意识） 134
- Section I Accounting Study（会计学习） 134
  - 6.1 Financial Documents（财务文件） 134

6.2　Cash-Flow Problems（现金流问题） 136
  6.3　Collecting Overdue Account Letters（催收账款信函） 136
  6.4　The Profit and Loss Account（损益账户） 143
  6.5　Annual Report: Chairman's Statement（年度报告） 144
  6.6　Setting up in Business（创立企业） 147
 Section II　Review & Exercises（复习与练习） 151
  Summary 151
  Questions 152
  Solved Problems 154
 Section III　Reading Material（阅读材料） 156
  Statement of Cash Flows 156
Appendix 1　Accounting Law of the People's Republic of China（中华人民共和国会计法） 162
　　　　　　Accounting Standard for Business Enterprises: Basic Standard
　　　　　　（企业会计准则——基本准则） 168
Appendix 2　Glossary（专业词汇总表） 179
Appendix 3　Key to Exercises（练习参考答案） 189
Appendix 4　资产负债表（一） 216
　　　　　　资产负债表（二） 219
　　　　　　现金流量表（一） 221
　　　　　　现金流量表（二） 224
　　　　　　损益表 226

Chapter 1 The Fundamental Accounting Concepts and Principles

（会计概述）

导学： 会计（accounting）被定义为一种确认、计量和沟通经济信息的过程，它用来向用户提供经济管理方面的信息，为其作出判断、进行决策提供必要的依据。一个企业的财务状况是由资产对负债和资本的关系来表示的。资产（assets）是指企业所拥有或控制的能以货币计量的经济资源。负债（liabilities）是指企业所承担的能以货币计量、需要以资产或劳务清偿的债务。资本（capital）是企业投资人对企业净资产的所有权，也称之为业主权益（owner's equity）。资产、负债和资本这三个基本要素由会计等式连接起来，即：资产 = 负债 + 资本。

 Section I Accounting Study（会计学习）

1.1 Introduction

（引言）

Do you use accounting? Yes, we all use accounting information in one form or another. For example, when you think about buying a house, you use accounting-type information to determine whether you can afford it and whether to lease or buy. Similarly, when you decide to go to college, you considered the costs (the tuition, textbooks, and so on). Most likely, you also considered the benefits (the ability to obtain a higher-paying job or a more desirable job).

Is accounting important to you? Yes, accounting is important in your personal life as well as your career, even though you may not become an accountant. For example, assume that you are the owner or manager of a small restaurant and are considering opening another restaurant in a neighboring town. Accounting information about the restaurant will be a major factor in your deciding whether to open the new restaurant and the bank's deciding whether to finance the expansion.

Our primary objective in this text is to illustrate basic accounting concepts that will help you to make good personal and business decisions.

What is Accounting

Accounting may be defined as a process of identifying, measuring and communicating economic information to permit informed judgments and decisions by users of information.

Accounting has often been called the "language of business". Every part of business is affected by accounting. Management of a business depends on financial information in making sound operational decisions. Stockholders must have financial information in order to measure management's performance and to evaluate their own holdings. Potential investors need financial data in order to compare prospective investments. Creditors must consider the financial strength of a business before permitting it to borrow funds. Also, many laws require that extensive financial information be reported to the various governmental agencies at least annually.

Brief History of Accounting

The origins of accounting are generally attributed to the work of Luca Pacioli, an Italian mathematician. In one of his text, Pacioli described a system to ensure that financial information was recorded efficiently and accurately.

With the advent of the industrial age in the nineteenth century and, later, the emergence of large corporations, a separation of the owners from the managers of businesses took place. As a result, the need to report the financial status of the enterprise became more important, to ensure that managers acted in accord with owners' wishes. Also, transactions between businesses became more complex, making necessary improved approaches for reporting financial information.

Our economy has now evolved into a post-industrial age—the information age—in which many "products" are information services. The computer has been the driver of the information age.

Two Major Specialized Fields in Accounting

Financial Accounting and Managerial Accounting are two major specialized fields in Accounting. *Financial Accounting* mainly reports information on the financial position and operating results of a business for both the external users and the business as well. Financial Accounting information is summarized and communicated to the interested users in the form of financial reports which are primarily composed of financial statements. They will be prepared and pu at least annually to the external users.

Managerial Accounting provides special information for the managers of a company ranging from broad, long-range plans to detailed explanations of a specific operation result. Therefore, Managerial Accounting information focuses in the parts of a company and is reported timely as required for the efficient decisions. Emphasis on Managerial Accounting has increased in recent years as a result of the utilization of computers and sophisticated tools.

This book will focus on Financial Accounting.

Bookkeeping and Accounting

Persons with little knowledge of accounting may fail to understand the difference between accounting and bookkeeping. Bookkeeping means the recording of transactions, the record-making phase of accounting. The recording of transactions tend to be mechanical and repetitive, it is only a small part of the field of accounting and probably the simplest part. Accounting includes not only the maintenance of accounting records, but also the design of efficient accounting systems, the performance of audits, the development of forecasts, income tax work, and the interpretation of accounting information. A person might become a reasonably proficient bookkeeper in a few weeks or months; however, to become a professional accountant requires several years of study and experience. Bookkeeping and accounting techniques will both be discussed.

Bookkeeper and Accountant

An individual who earns a living by recording the financial activities of a business is known as a ***bookkeeper***, while the process of classifying and summarizing business transactions and interpreting their effects is accomplished by the ***accountant***. The bookkeeper is concerned with techniques involving the recording of transactions, and the accountant's objective is the use of data for interpretation.

 New Words, Phrases and Special Terms

accountant	n.	会计（员）
accounting	n.	会计（学）
accounting concept		会计概念
accounting information		会计信息
accounting system		会计制度，会计系统
advent	n.	（尤指不寻常的人或事）出现，到来
annually	adv.	每年地，年度地

approach	n.	方法，步骤
attribute (to)		把……归因于……
audit	vt.	审计
be composed of		由……组成
benefit	n.	利益，好处
bookkeeper	n.	簿记员
bookkeeping	n.	簿记
classify	vt.	把……分类
communicate	v.	传递，沟通
contemporary	n.	同时代的人
creditor	n.	债权人
desirable	adj.	需要的，合意的，令人想要的
distinguish	v.	区别，辨别，认别
emergence	n.	浮现，露出，出现
enterprise	n.	企业
evaluate	vt.	评价，评估
evolve	v.	（使）发展，（使）进展
finance	vt.	供给……经费，负担经费
financial accounting		财务会计
financial information		财务信息
financial position		财务状况
financial report		财务报告
fundamental	adj.	基础的，基本的
identify	vt.	识别，鉴别
illustrate	vt.	举例说明，图解，阐明
in accord with		与……一致
income tax		所得税
interpret	vt.	解释，说明
investor	n.	投资者
lease	v.	出租
long-range plan		长期计划
mathematician	n.	数学家
managerial accounting		管理会计
measure	vt.	计量，衡量
obtain	vt.	获得，得到

operating results		经营成果
operational	adj.	操作的，运作的
origin	n.	起源，由来，起因
principle	n.	法则，原则
potential	adj.	潜在的，可能的
prepare	vt.	编制
profession	n.	职业
proficient	adj.	熟练的
prospective	adj.	预期的
record	vt. n.	记录
operational	adj.	可靠的，合理的
sophisticated	adj.	复杂的，完善的
sound	adj.	可靠的，合理的
specialized	adj.	专门的，专科的
status	n.	身份，地位，情形，状况
stockholder	n.	股东
strength	n.	实力
summarize	vt.	汇总
transaction	n.	交易，业务
tuition	n.	学费
utilization	n.	利用

 Notes

1. Management of a business depends on financial information in making sound operational decisions.
企业管理人员在进行有效的经营决策时要依赖于财务信息。

2. Creditors must consider the financial strength of a business before permitting it to borrow funds.
债权人在同意给企业贷款前，必然要考虑企业的财务实力。

3. Also, many laws require that extensive financial information be reported to the various governmental agencies at least annually.
许多法律条规亦规定企业应至少每年向不同的政府部门报告全面的财务信息。

4. The origins of accounting are generally attributed to the work of Luca Pacioli, an Italian mathematician.
会计的起源通常归因于意大利数学家卢卡·帕乔利的著作。

5. In *one of his text*, Pacioli described a system to ensure that financial information was recorded efficiently and accurately.

one of his text 指 1494 年卢卡·帕乔利在总结前人的实践基础上出版的《算术、几何、比及比例概要》。在第三部分的簿记中详细论述了借贷记账方法，提出"借"、"贷"符号，会计基本恒等式，财产清算方法，日记账、分录账、总账登记方法，以及试算平衡方法。卢卡·帕乔利因此被称为"近代会计之父"。

6. Financial Accounting and Managerial Accounting are two major *specialized fields in Accounting*.

specialized fields in accounting 会计专业领域。除了财务会计和管理会计这一分类外，根据提供财务信息的目的，会计还可以划分为企业会计（private accounting）、公共会计（public accounting）、税务会计（tax accounting）、非营利组织会计（not-for-profit accounting）、成本会计（cost accounting）、社会会计（social accounting）等。

7. They will be prepared and published at least annually to the *external users*.

external users 外部使用者，相对于提供信息的企业或内部使用者（internal users）之外的信息使用者。

8. Financial Accounting information is summarized and communicated to the interested users in the form of financial reports which are primarily composed of financial statements.

财务会计以财务报告的形式把信息归类，并传递给利益相关者，而财务报表是财务报告的主要组成部分。

9. ***Managerial Accounting*** provides special information for the managers of a company ranging from broad, long-range plans to detailed explanations of a specific operation result.

管理会计向企业管理人员提供专门信息，范围涉及长期的总体计划到某一具体经营成果的详尽解释。

10. Bookkeeping means the recording of transactions, the record-making phase of accounting.

簿记就是记录经济业务，是会计的记账阶段。

11. Accounting includes not only the maintenance of accounting records, but also the design of efficient accounting systems, the performance of audits, the development of forecasts, income tax work, and the interpretation of accounting information.

会计不仅包括会计记录，还包括有效会计制度的设计，审计、预算、所得税的计算，以及会计信息的诠释。

12. **financial reports** 财务报告，又称会计报告，是会计程序的总结性文件，是准确反映企业财务状况和营利能力的报告。财务报告是会计过程的最终成果。财务报告由财务报表、报表附注（Notes to financial statements）、会计政策（Accounting Policy）、会计政策变动（Changes in accounting policy）等部分组成，其中以财务报表为主体。企业应编制的财务报表包括资产负债表、损益表、现金流量表三种基本报表，其他报表为基本报表的副表。

1.2　The Accounting Profession
（会计职业）

What would you do if you join the accounting profession? You probably would work in one of three major fields—public accounting, private accounting or not-for-profit accounting.

Public Accounting

In public accounting, you would offer expert service to the general public in much the same way that a doctor serves patients and a lawyer serves clients. Public accounting firms are organizations which offer a variety of accounting services to the public. These firms vary in size from one-person practices to large, international organizations with several thousand professional accountants.

Most of the people in public accounting are licensed as ***certified public accountants (CPAs)***. Thus, public accounting firms often are called ***CPA firms***.

The primary services offered by CPA firms include auditing, taxation and management consulting.

A major portion of public accounting involves ***auditing***. In this area, a certified public accountant (CPA) examines the financial statements of companies and expresses an opinion as to the fairness of presentation. When the presentation is fair, users consider the statements to be reliable.

Taxation is another major area of public accounting. The work performed by tax specialists includes tax advice and planning, preparing tax returns, and representing clients before governmental agencies such as the Internal Revenue Service.

A third area in public accounting is ***management consulting***. Many CPA firms offer their clients a wide range of management consulting services. It ranges from the installing of basic accounting systems to helping companies determine whether they should use the space shuttle for high-tech research and development projects. For example, a CPA firm might be engaged to study the feasibility of installing a computer-based accounting system, of introducing a new product line, or of merging with another company. The fact that business executives often seek their accountants' advice on a wide range of problems illustrates the relevance of accounting information to virtually all business decisions.

Private Accounting

Instead of working in public accounting, you might choose to be an employee of a business enterprise. In private (or managerial) accounting, you would be involved in one of the following activities.

General accounting—recording daily transactions and preparing financial statements and related information.

Cost accounting—determining the cost of producing specific products. Knowing the cost of a particular product is vital to the efficient management of a business. For example, an automobile manufacturer needs to know the cost of each type of car produced. Knowing the cost of each manufacturing process or the cost of any business operation is also essential to making sound business decisions. The phrase of accounting particular concerned with collecting and interpreting cost data is called *Cost Accounting*.

Budgeting—assisting management in quantifying goals concerning revenues, costs of goods sold, and operating expenses. A budget (financial forecast) is a plan of financial operations for some future period expressed in monetary terms. By using a budget, management is able to make comparisons between *planned operations* and *actual results achieved*. A budget is thus an attempt to preview operating results before the actual transactions have taken place.

Accounting information systems—designing both manual and computerized data processing systems. Although the same basic accounting principles are applicable to all types of business, each enterprise requires an individually tailored *financial information system*. This system includes accounting forms, records, instruction manuals, flow charts, computer programs, and reports to fit the particular needs of the business. Designing an accounting system and putting it into operation constitute a specialized phase of accounting.

Tax accounting—preparing tax returns and doing tax planning for the company. As income taxes have increased in importance and the determination of taxable income has become more complex, both internal accountants and independent public accountants have devoted more time to problems of taxation. Although many companies rely largely on CPA firms for tax planning and the preparation of income tax returns, large companies also maintain their own tax departments.

Internal auditing—reviewing the company's operations to see if they comply with management policies and evaluating the efficiency of operations. Most large corporations maintain staffs of *internal auditors* with the responsibility of evaluating the efficiency of operations and determining whether company policies are being followed consistently in all divisions of the corporation. The internal auditor, in contrast to the independent auditor or CPA, is not responsible for determining the overall fairness of the company's annual financial statements.

Not-for-Profit Accounting

Like business that exists to make a profit, not-for-profit organizations also need sound financial reporting and control. Donors to such organizations as the United Way, the Ford Foundation, and the Red Cross want information about how well the organization has met its financial objectives and whether continued support is justified. Hospitals, colleges, and universities must make decisions about allocating funds. Locals, state, and federal governmental units provide financial information to legislators, citizens, employees, and creditors. At the federal level, the largest employers of accountants are the Internal Revenue Service, the General Accounting Office, the Federal Bureau of Investigation, and the Securities and Exchange Commission.

New Words, Phrases and Special Terms

allocate	vt.	分配，分派
applicable	adj.	可适用的，可应用的
automobile	n.	（美）汽车
certified public accountant (CPA)		注册会计师
comparison	n.	比较，对照
comply with		同意，遵守
computerize	vt.	用计算机处理，使计算机化
consulting	adj.	商议的，咨询的
CPA firm		会计师事务所
donor	n.	捐赠人
enterprise	n.	企业
executive	n.	管理人员，行政部门
feasibility	n.	可行性
Federal Bureau of Investigation (FBI)		美国联邦调查局
financial forecast		财务预测
financial statement		财务报表
Ford Foundation		（美国）福特基金
General Accounting Office		（美）审计总局，会计总署
high-tech	n.	高科技
Internal Revenue Service		（美）国内税收署
introduce	vt.	引进，引入
legislator	n.	立法者
management consulting		管理咨询
manufacturer	n.	制造业者，厂商
merge	v.	合并，结合
monetary	adj.	货币的
not-for-profit accounting		非营利组织会计
operating result		业务成果，运营结果
overall	adj.	全部的，全面的

particular	adj.	特殊的，特别的
preview	vt.	事先查看，预展
private accounting		企业会计，私用会计
product line		生产线
public accounting		公共会计
quantify	vt.	确定数量
Red Cross		红十字会
relevance	n.	中肯，适当
reliable	adj.	可靠的
securities and Exchange Commission		证券交易管理委员会
space shuttle		航天飞机
tailored	adj.	量身定做的
taxation	n.	征税
tax return		纳税申报单
United Way		美国联合劝募会
variety	n.	变化，多样性
virtually	adv.	事实上，实质上
vital	adj.	至关重要的，所必需的

 Notes

1. A budget is a plan of financial operations for some future period expressed in monetary terms.

财务预算是用货币形式表述的未来期间财务活动的计划。

2. By using a budget, management is able to make comparisons between *planned operations* and *actual results achieved*.

通过预算，管理部门可以将实际完成的情况与计划进行对比。

3. *Accounting information systems*—designing both manual and computerized data processing systems.

A manually maintained bookkeeping system 手工簿记系统。会计记账程序已由原始的手工操作发展为机械化操作，直至今日的计算机化数据处理（computerized data processing）。尽管如此，会计的基本原理是一样的。本书以手工簿记为例说明基本的会计记账程序。

4. This system includes accounting forms, records, instruction manuals, flow charts, computer programs, and reports to fit the particular needs of the business.

该（财务信息）系统包括适应特定企业需要的会计表格、会计账簿、指导手册、流程图、计算机程序和报告。

5. As income taxes have increased in importance and the determination of taxable income has become more

complex, both internal accountants and independent public accountants have devoted more time to problems of taxation.

随着所得税重要性的增长以及确定应税所得越来越复杂，企业内部的会计师和独立的公共会计师都把更多的时间用于（处理）纳税问题。

6. Most large corporations maintain staffs of ***internal auditors*** with the responsibility of evaluating the efficiency of operations and determining whether company policies are being followed consistently in all divisions of the corporation.

多数大公司都有内部审计师，他们负责评价经营效率并确认公司的每个部门是否都始终如一地遵循了公司的政策。

7. The internal auditor, in contrast to the independent auditor or CPA, is not responsible for determining the overall fairness of the company's annual financial statements.

与独立审计师或注册会计师相反，内部审计师并不能负责认定公司的年度财务报表是否公正合理。

8. ..., and representing clients before governmental agencies such as the *Internal Revenue Service*.

美国国内税收署是完成大量会计工作的政府机构之一。它掌握了由个人和公司填写的成百万的所得税申报单，并经常对这些所得税申报单和作为其基础的会计记录执行审计职能。

9. Donors to such organizations as the United Way, the Ford Foundation, and the Red Cross want...

（1）United Way 联合劝募会是美国最大的一家慈善组织和联合劝募系统（United Way System）。联合劝募是一个以社区为基础的系统，其组织遍及全世界各城市与国家。它是一个自给自足的系统，将来自政府、企业及社会各阶层的人结合起来，共同讨论人类的健康和福利问题，并且提出解决之道。

（2）Ford Foundation 福特基金会是一个致力于国际和平和改善人类福利的私人慈善机构。它们的工作主要是向政府和非政府机构提供资助，资助研究、培训、能力建设、试验和开发性项目。另外，此基金会也提供一些个人资助。

（3）Red Cross 国际红十字会从 1863 年诞生，已经发展成为当今的一个行动组织，它的工作遍及世界各地。它的工作是对因武装冲突或因敌对者的行为而丧失保护的人采取人道主义行动。

10. Securities and Exchange Commission 证券交易管理委员会是与会计有密切联系的另一家政府机构。证券交易管理委员会负责确立关于财务报表的内容及应遵循的编报标准的要求。所有将把证券销售给公众的公司都必须每年填写由证券交易管理委员会审计的财务报表以满足这些要求。

11. financial statement 财务报表

基本的财务报表有：资产负债表（balance sheet）；损益表（income statement）；现金流量表（statement of cash flows）。

1.3　Accounting as an Information System
（会计信息系统）

Traditionally, we considered skilled worker and staff, materials, money and machines as the main resources of an organization, but today we become aware that information is an additional important resource without which organizational objectives can not be achieved. The design of an effective information system is so important in recent years that it has become a specialized activity for professionals. Accounting is an information system necessitated by the great complexity of modern business, which is designed to record, sort and summarize systematically financial and other economic information related to business transactions and events, stated in monetary terms.

One of the most important functions of accounting is to accumulate and report financial position and the results of its operations to its interested users. These users include managers, stockholders, banks and other creditors, government agencies, investment advisors, and the general public. To meet the needs of the external users, a framework of accounting standards, principles and procedures known as "generally accepted accounting principles" have been developed to insure the relevance and reliability of the accounting information contained in these external financial reports. The subdivision of the accounting process that produces these external reports is referred to as financial accounting.

Another important function of accounting is to provide the management inside an organization with the accounting information needed in the organization's internal decision-making, which relates to planning, control, and evaluation within an organization. For example, budgets are prepared under the directions of a company's controller on an annual basis and express the desires and goals of the company's management. A performance report is supplied to help a manger focus his attention on problems or opportunities that might otherwise go unnoticed. Furthermore, cost-benefit data will be needed by a company's management in deciding among the alternatives of reducing price, increasing advertising, or doing both in attempt to maintain its market shares. The process of generating and analyzing such accounting information for internal decision-making is often referred to as managerial accounting and the related information reports being prepared are called internal management reports. As contrasted with financial accounting, a managerial accounting information system provides both historical and estimated information that is relevant to the specific plans on more frequent basis. And managerial accounting is not governed by generally accepted accounting principles.

The growth of organizations, changes in technology, government regulation, and the globalization of economy during the twentieth century have spurred the development of accounting. As a result, a number of specialized fields of accounting have evolved in addition to financial accounting and managerial accounting, which include auditing, cost accounting, tax accounting, budgetary accounting, governmental and not-for-profit accounting, human resources accounting, environmental accounting, social accounting, international accounting, etc. For example, tax accounting encompasses the preparation of tax returns and the consideration of the tax consequences of proposed business transactions or alternative courses of action. Governmental and not-for-profit accounting specializes in recording and reporting the transactions of various governmental units and other not-for-profit organizations. International accounting is concerned with the special problems associated with the international trade of multinational business organizations. All forms of accounting, in the end, provide information to the related users and help them make decisions.

 New Words, Phrases and Special Terms

accumulate	vt.	累积
accounting process		会计程序，会计处理过程
alternative	n.	可供选择的办法，事物
associated	adj.	联合的，关联的
be concerned with		与……有关
budget	n.	预算
budgetary accounting		预算会计
complexity	n.	复杂性
consequence	n.	结果
controller	n.	主计长，总会计师
cost accounting		成本会计
cost-benefit data		成本－效益数据
decision-making	n.	决策
encompass	vt.	包围，包含或包括某事物
environmental accounting		环境会计
framework	n.	构架，框架，结构
function	n.	作用，职能
generally accepted accounting principles (GAAP)		公认会计原则
generate	v.	产生，引起
globalization	n.	全球化
governmental and not-for-profit accounting		政府及非营利组织会计
human resources accounting		人力资源会计
in addition to		除……之外
information system		信息系统
international accounting		国际会计

market share		市场份额，市场占有率
modern business		现代企业
multinational	adj.	多国的，跨国公司的
necessitate	vt.	使成为必要
performance	n.	工作业绩
performance report		业绩报告
prior to		在……之前
professional	n.	专业人员
regulation	n.	规则，规章
social accounting		社会会计
specialize (in)	vi.	专攻，专门研究
spur	vt.	刺激
subdivision	n.	分支
systematically	adv.	系统地，有系统地
tax accounting		税务会计

 Notes

1. Traditionally, we considered skilled worker and staff, materials, money and machines as the main resources of an organization, but today we become aware that information is an additional important resource without which organizational objectives can not be achieved.

过去我们认为，熟练员工、物资、货币和设备是企业的主要资源，但如今日益认识到信息是另一种重要的资源，没有信息，企业的目标就不能实现。

2. The design of an effective information system is so important in recent years that it has become a specialized activity for professionals.

近年来，人们越来越重视有效的信息系统的设计，致使信息系统设计已成为一项由专业人员完成的专门化的工作。

3. Accounting is an information system necessitated by the great complexity of modern business, which is designed to record, sort and summarize systematically financial and other economic information related to business transactions and events, stated in monetary terms.

会计由于现代企业的巨大复杂性而成为必要的信息系统，它以货币为计量单位，系统地对企业的财务和其他经济活动加以记录、归类和汇总，并分析、解释其结果。

4. One of the most important functions of accounting is to accumulate and report financial position and the results of its operations to its interested users.

会计最重要的职能之一是向有利害关系的使用者积累并报告组织内部的财务状况和经营成果。

5. To meet the needs of the external users, a framework of accounting standards, principles and procedures known as "generally accepted accounting principles" have been developed to insure the relevance and reliability of the accounting information contained in these external financial reports.

为了满足外部使用者的需求，一套包括会计准则、会计原则和会计程序的框架，即"公认会计原则"产生了，目的是保证这些对外报告提供的财务信息具有相关性和可靠性。

6. Another important function of accounting is to provide the management inside an organization with the accounting information needed in the organization's internal decision-making, which relates to planning, control, and evaluation within an organization.

会计的另一个重要职能是向某一组织的管理当局提供该组织内部决策所需的会计信息，这些决策包括组织计划、控制和评价。

7. As contrasted with financial accounting, a managerial accounting information system provides both historical and estimated information that is relevant to the specific plans on more frequent basis.

与财务会计不同，管理会计信息系统会更多地提供与具体计划相关的历史信息和预测信息。

8. The growth of organizations, changes in technology, government regulation, and the globalization of economy during the twentieth century have spurred the development of accounting.

20世纪各类组织的成长、技术的变革、政府的规章制度以及经济全球化都推动了会计的发展。

9. For example, tax accounting encompasses the preparation of tax returns and the consideration of the tax consequences of proposed business transactions or alternative courses of action.

比如说，税务会计包含纳税申报以及研究企业经济业务或不同措施可能产生的纳税影响。

10. controller 主计长，总会计师

中型或大型企业的总会计师称为主计长。他管理会计职员的工作，也是企业高层管理人员，承担管理企业、确定企业目标并监督这些目标完成的任务。

※1.4 Accounting Principles and Concepts
（会计原则和概念）

The Definition of Accounting Principle

The accounting profession has developed standards that are generally accepted and universally practiced. This common set of standards is called ***generally accepted accounting principles (GAAP)***. Accounting principles are also referred to as standards, assumptions, postulates, and concepts. These standards indicate how to report economic events.

Assumptions of Financial Accounting

The most fundamental assumptions underlying the accounting process are:

Accounting Entity. One of the basic principles of accounting is that information is complied for a clearly defined accounting entity. Each business venture is a separate unit, accounting separately. Therefore, financial statements are identified as belonging to a particular business entity.

Going Concern. An underlying assumption in accounting is that an accounting entity will continue in operation for a period of time sufficient to carry out its existing commitments. Any foreseeable suspension of operations must be disclosed on the financial statements. The process of termination, which occurs when a company ceases business operations and sells its assets, is called liquidation. If liquidation appears likely, the going concern assumption is no longer valid.

Accounting Period. We assume an indefinite life for most accounting entities. But accountants are asked to measure operating progress and changes in economic position at relatively short time intervals during this indefinite life. Users of financial statements need periodic measurements for decision-making purposes.

The need for frequent measurements creates many of the accountant's most challenging problems. Dividing the life of an enterprise into time segments, such as a year or a quarter of a year, requires numerous estimates and assumptions.

Stable Dollar Assumption. The stable dollar assumption means that money is used as the basic measuring unit for financial reporting. Money is the common denominator in which accounting measurements are made and summarized. The dollar, or any other monetary unit, represents a unit of value; that is, it reflects ability to command goods and services. Implicit in the use of money as a measuring unit is the assumption that the dollar is a stable unit of value, just as the mile is a stable unit of distance and acre is a stable unit of area.

The Principles of Financial Accounting

The Objectivity Principle. The term *objective* refers to measurements that are unbiased and subject to verification by independent experts. Accountants rely on various kinds of evidence to support their financial measurements, but they seek always the most objective evidence available. Invoices, contracts, paid checks, and physical counts of inventory are examples of objective evidence.

Asset Valuation: The Cost Principle. Both the balance sheet and the income statement are affected by the cost principle. Assets are initially recorded in the accounts at cost, and no adjustment is made to this valuation in later periods. At the time an asset is originally acquired, cost represents the "fair market value" of the goods or services exchanged, as evidenced by an arm's-length transaction. With the passage of time, however, the fair market value of such assets as land and buildings may change greatly from their historical cost. These later changes in fair market value generally have been ignored in the accounts, and the assets have continued to be valued in the balance sheet at historical cost.

Measuring Revenue: The Realization Principle. When should revenue be recognized? In most cases, the realization principle indicates that revenue should be recognized at the time goods are sold or services are rendered. At this point the business has essentially completed the earning process and the sales value of the goods or services can be measured objectively. At any time prior to sale, the ultimate sales value of the goods or services sold can only be estimated.

Measuring Expenses: The Matching Principle. The measurement of expenses occurs in two stages: (1) measuring the cost of goods and services that will be consumed or expire in generating revenue and (2) determining when the goods and services acquired have contributed to revenue and their cost thus becomes an expense. The second aspect of the measurement process is often referred to as matching costs and revenue and is fundamental to the accrual basis of accounting.

The Consistency Principle. The principle of consistency implies that a particular accounting method, once adopted, will not be changed from period to period. This assumption is important because it assists users of financial statements in interpreting changes in financial position and changes in net income.

The principle of consistency does not mean that a company should never make a change in its accounting methods. In fact, a company should make a change if a proposed new accounting method will provide more useful information than does the method presently in use. But when a significant change in accounting methods does occur, the fact that a change has been made and the dollar effects of the change should be fully disclosed in the financial statements.

The Disclosure Principle. Adequate disclosure means that all material and relevant facts concerning financial position and the results of operations are communicated to users. This can be accomplished either in the financial statements or in the notes accompanying the statements. Such disclosure should make the financial statements more useful and less subject to misinterpretation.

The key point to bear in mind is that the supplementary information should be relevant to the interpretation of the financial statements.

Materiality. The term materiality refers to the relative importance of an item or event. Accountants are primarily concerned with significant information and are not overly concerned with those items that have little effect on financial statements.

Materiality of an item may develop not only on its account but also on its nature.

Organizations Influencing Accounting Practice

A number of organizations exist in U.S.A. that are concerned with the formulation of accounting principles. The most prominent among them is the Financial Accounting Standards Board. The FASB, organized in

1973, is a nongovernmental body whose pronouncements have the force of dictating authoritative rules for the general practice of financial accounting. Before the creation of the FASB, the Accounting Principles Board of the American Institute of Certified Public Accountants fulfilled the function of formulating accounting principles.

 New Words, Phrases and Special Terms

accounting entity		会计主体
accounting period		会计期间
accounting principle		会计原则
Accounting Principles Board (APB)		会计原则委员会
accrual	n.	获利,利息,自然增长
accrual basis		权责发生制
acre	n.	英亩
American Institute of Certified Public Accountants (AICPA)		美国注册会计师协会
arm's-length		正常交易关系
asset valuation		资产价值
assumption	n.	假设
authoritative	adj.	权威的
business venture		企业
business operation		营业
cease	v.	停止
commitment	n.	允诺,义务
compile	v.	搜集,汇集
concept	n.	概念
consistency principle		一致性原则
cost principle		成本原则
denominator	n.	分母,共同特征,标准
disclose	vt.	披露,透露

disclosure principle		披露原则
economic unit		经济单位
economic activity		经济活动
engage in		参加，从事
expire	v.	期满，终止
Financial Accounting Standards Board (FASB)		财务会计准则委员会
financial position		财务状况
foreseeable	adj.	预见的，可见的
formulation	n.	公式化，有系统的阐述，模式
full disclosure		充分披露
going-concern assumption		持续经营假设
implicit	adj.	暗示的
indefinite	adj.	模糊的，不确定的
interpret	vt.	解释，说明
liquidation	n.	清算
matching principle		配比原则
materiality	n.	重要性
measuring expense		计量费用
measuring revenue		计量收入
monetary principle		货币原则
net income		净收益
nongovernmental body		非政府机构
objectivity	n.	客观性
partnership	n.	合伙企业
periodic	adj.	周期的，定期的
postulate	n.	假定
pronouncement	n.	声明
proprietorship	n.	独资企业
realization principle		实现原则
revenue	n.	收入，收益
stable	adj.	稳定的
subject to		使服从
suspension	n.	暂停，停止支付
termination	n.	终止
unbiased	adj.	无偏见的

underlying	adj.	在下面的，根本的
valid	adj.	有效的
valuation	n.	评价，计算
verification	n.	确认，查证

Notes

1. One of the basic principles of accounting is that information is complied for a clearly defined accounting entity.

会计基本原则之一是会计信息的搜集处理应基于一个明确界定的会计主体。

2. An underlying assumption in accounting is that an accounting entity will continue in operation for a period of time sufficient to carry out its existing commitments.

会计的一个基本假设是会计主体在一定时期内"持续经营"并履行存续期间的各种义务。

3. But accountants are asked to measure operating progress and changes in economic position at relatively short time intervals during this indefinite life.

但在持续的经营状况下，会计人员要人为地区分若干时间间隔来衡量经营进展和经济状况的变化。

4. Money is the common denominator in which accounting measurements are made and summarized.

货币是进行会计计量和汇总的共同尺度。

5. The dollar, or any other monetary unit, represents a unit of value; that is, it reflects ability to command goods and services.

美元，或者任何其他货币单位，代表一个价值单位，也就是说，它反映拥有商品和劳务的能力。

6. Implicit in the use of money as a measuring unit is the assumption that the dollar is a stable unit of value, just as the mile is a stable unit of distance and acre is a stable unit of area.

无疑地，在用货币作计量单位时，（我们）假设美元是一个稳定的计价单位，就像英里是一个固定的距离单位，而英亩是一个固定的面积单位一样。

7. The term objective refers to measurements that are unbiased and subject to verification by independent experts.

对于计量来说，"客观性"这个术语是指公平的，并且须经独立的专家来认定的。

8. Assets are initially recorded in the accounts at cost, and no adjustment is made to this valuation in later periods.

资产是按取得成本记录在账户中的，这个价值在以后的会计期间不做调整。

9. At the time an asset is originally acquired, cost represents the "fair market value" of the goods or services exchanged, as evidenced by an arm's-length transaction.

在最初获得一项资产时，成本代表交换商品或劳务的"公平市价"，并作为一项交易是否正常的判断依据。

acquisition cost 取得成本，也称为 original cost（原始成本），是固定资产的计价基础。例如，某企业购置设备，该设备的成本包括购买价和运输费、保险费、安装费等。

10. At this point the business has essentially completed the earning process and the sales value of the goods or services can be measured objectively.

此刻企业已基本完成了营利过程，而且商品或劳务的销售价值可以客观地计量。

11. In most cases, the realization principle indicates that revenue should be recognized at the time goods are sold or services are rendered.

在大多数情况下，实现原则是指收入应该在出售商品或提供劳务的那一刻确认。

12. The measurement of expenses occurs in two stages: (1) measuring the cost of goods and services that will be consumed or expire in generating revenue and (2) determining when the goods and services acquired have contributed to revenue and their cost thus becomes an expense.

费用的计量发生在两个阶段：(1) 在获得收入时计量消费或消耗掉的商品和劳务的成本；(2) 在确定获得的商品和劳务产生收入时确认其成本为费用。

13. The second aspect of the measurement process is often referred to as *matching costs and revenue* and is fundamental to the accrual basis of accounting.

计量过程的第二方面也常称为成本和收入配比，而且它是会计权责发生制的基础。

14. Adequate disclosure means that all material and relevant facts concerning financial position and the results of operations are communicated to users.

充分披露就是与财务状况和经营成果所有相关重要信息都要传递给使用者。

15. Accountants are primarily concerned with significant information and are not overly concerned with those items that have little effect on financial statements.

会计人员首先关注的是重要信息，而不会过度关心那些对财务报表影响极小的项目。

16. accounting entity 会计主体

一个会计主体就是任意一个可以掌握财源并从事经济活动的经济单位。一个人可以是一个会计主体，一个企业（无论是独资、合伙或股份公司）也可以是会计主体；政府机构可以是会计主体，非营利组织也可以是会计主体。

1.5 Basic Elements of Financial Position: The Accounting Equation
（会计基本要素：会计等式）

Accounting Elements

The three basic accounting elements are assets, liabilities and capital. They exist in every business entity.

Assets. The assets of a business are, in general, the properties or economic resources owned by the business. Assets may have definite physical form such as cash, buildings, machinery, equipment or merchandise. Assets may also exist in the form of valuable legal claims or rights such as amounts due from customers, investments in government bonds and patent rights.

Liabilities. Liabilities are amounts owed to outsiders, such as notes payable and accounts payable.

Capital. Capital is the interest of the owners in an enterprise and also it is known as owner's equity. It is equal to total assets minus total liabilities. If there are no liabilities, the capital is equal to the total amount of the assets. Capital is increased with revenue, and decreased by expense or an owner's withdrawal.

The Accounting Equation

The financial condition or position of a business enterprise is represented by the relationship of assets to liabilities and capital. These three basic elements are connected by a fundamental relationship called ***balance sheet equation***, sometimes called simply ***the accounting equation***. This equation expresses the equality of the assets on one side with the claims of the creditors and owners on the other side:

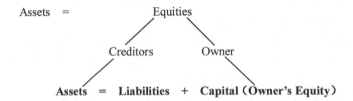

Assets = Liabilities + Capital (Owner's Equity)

This equation shows assets are equal to equities. Equities are divided into liabilities and capital (owner's equity). When the amounts of any two of these elements (assets, liabilities or capital) are known, the third can be calculated. The following are variations of the accounting equation:

Capital = Assets − Liabilities
Liabilities = Assets − Capital
Liabilities + Capital = Assets

Any activity of a business that affects the accounting equation is a ***transaction***. Buying and selling assets, performing services and borrowing money are common business transactions. The effect of any transaction on the accounting equation may be indicated by increasing or decreasing a specific asset, liability or capital element. The accounting equation holds at all times over the life of the business. When a transaction occurs, the total assets of the business may change, but the equation will remain in balance.

Three Additional Items

To complete our discussion of the accounting equation, three additional items must be covered: revenue, expense and owner's withdrawal.

The term *revenue* generally means an increase in assets because a service was rendered. Revenue is one of the two ways that capital (owner's equity) can be increased:

(1) The owner may invest cash. Such an investment increases both assets and capital.

(2) Revenue earned from providing goods or services to customers also increases capital.

When revenue is earned, the assets are increased (normally cash or accounts receivable), and capital is increased too.

The term *expense* generally means a decrease in assets (usually cash) or an increase in liabilities (usually accountant payable) in order to earn more revenue. Just like revenue, an expense directly affects the capital and is one of the two ways that capital (owner's equity) can be decreased:

(1) The owner may withdraw cash or other assets from the business. This type of transaction is charged to the owner's drawing account.

(2) Expenses incurred in operating the business also decrease capital.

Common examples of expenses are office rent, salaries of employees, telephone service, and many types of taxes.

If total revenue of the period exceeds total expenses, the result is called *net income*. On the other hand, if total expenses of the period exceed total revenue, the result is called *net loss*.

Illustrations

The accounting equation serves as the basis for the balance sheets, as illustrated in the following example.

Example 1

Assume that a business owned assets of $100,000, owed creditors $80,000, and owed the owner $20,000. The accounting equation would be:

$$\text{Assets} = \text{Liabilities} + \text{Capital}$$
$$\$100,000 \qquad \$80,000 \qquad \$20,000$$

Suppose that $6,000 was used to reduce liabilities and the balance remained in assets. The equation would then be:

$$\text{Assets} = \text{Liabilities} + \text{Capital}$$
$$\$104,000 \qquad \$74,000 \qquad \$30,000$$

In Example 1, the net changes in asset groups were discussed; in Example 2, we show how the accountant makes a meaningful record of a series of transactions, reconciling them step by step with the accounting equation.

Example 2

During the month of March, Mark Himes, Lawyer

(1) Invested $4,000 to open his practice.

(2) Bought office supplies (stationery, legal pads, pencils, and so on) for cash, $300.

(3) Bought office furniture from Stanley·Furniture Company on account, $2,000.

(4) Received $2,500 in fees earned during the month.

(5) Paid office rent for January, $500.

(6) Paid salary for part-time help, $200.

(7) Paid $1,200 to Stanley Furniture Company on account.

(8) After taking an inventory at the end of the month, Himes found that he had used $200 worth of supplies.

(9) Withdrew $400 for personal use.

These transactions might be analyzed and recorded as follows:

Transaction (1) **Mr. Himes invested $4,000 to open his practice.** Two accounts are
March 1 affected: the asset Cash is increased, and the capital of the firm is increased by the same amount.

	Assets	=	Liabilities	+	Capital
	Cash				Mark Himes, Capital
(1)	+$4,000	=		+	$4,000

Transaction (2) **Bought supplies for cash, $300.** In this case, Mr. Himes is substituting one
March 4 asset for another; he is receiving (+) the asset Supplies and paying out (−) the asset Cash. Note that the capital of $4,000 remains unchanged, and there is still equality.

	Assets		=	Liabilities	+	Capital
	Cash	+ Supplies				Mark Himes, Capital
	$4,000					$4,000
	−300	+$300				
(2)	$3,700 +	$300	=		+	$4,000

Chapter 1 The Fundamental Accounting Concepts and Principles（会计概述）

Transaction (3) Bought office furniture from Stanley Furniture Company on account,
March 5 **$2,000.** Mr. Himes is receiving the asset Furniture but is not paying for it with the asset Cash. Instead, he will owe the money to the Stanley Furniture Company. Therefore, he is liable for this amount in the future, thus creating the liability Accounts Payable.

	Assets					=	Liabilities	+	Capital
	Cash	+	Supplies	+	Furniture		Accounts Payable		Mark Himes, Capital
	$3,700		$300						$4,000
					+$2,000		+$2,000		
(3)	$3,700	+	$300	+	$2,000	=	$2,000	+	$4,000

Transaction (4) Received $2,500 in fees earned during the month. Because Mr. Himes
March 15   received $2,500, the asset Cash increased, and also his capital increased. It is important to note that he labels the $2,500 *fees income* (revenue) to show its origin.

	Assets					=	Liabilities	+	Capital
	Cash	+	Supplies	+	Furniture		Accounts Payable		Mark Himes, Capital
	$3,700		$300		$2,000		$2,000		$4,000
	+2,500								+2,500 Fees Income
(4)	$6,200	+	$300	+	$2,000	=	$2,000	+	$6,500

Transaction (5) Paid office rent for March, $500. When the word "paid" is stated, you
March 30   know it means a deduction from cash, since Mr. Himes is paying out his asset Cash. Payment of expense is a reduction of capital. It is termed *rent expense*.

	Assets					=	Liabilities	+	Capital
	Cash	+	Supplies	+	Furniture		Accounts Payable		Mark Himes, Capital
	$6,200		$300		$2,000		$2,000		$6,500
	−500								−500 Rent Expense
(5)	$5,700	+	$300	+	$2,000	=	$2,000	+	$6,000

Transaction (6) Paid salary for part-time help, $200. Again, the word "paid" means a
March 30   deduction of cash and a reduction in capital. This time it refers to *salaries expense*.

	Assets			=	Liabilities	+	Capital
	Cash +	Supplies +	Furniture		Accounts Payable		Mark Himes, Capital
	$5,700	$300	$2,000		$2,000		$6,000
	−200						−200 Salaries Expense
(6)	$5,500 +	$300 +	$2,000	=	$2,000		+$5,800

Transaction (7) Paid $1,200 to Stanley Furniture Company on account. Here Mr.
March 31   Himes is reducing the asset Cash because he is paying $1,200, and he is also reducing the liability Accounts Payable. He will now owe $1,200 less.

	Assets			=	Liabilities	+	Capital
	Cash +	Supplies +	Furniture		Accounts Payable		Mark Himes, Capital
	$5,500	$300	$2,000		$2,000		$6,000
	−1,200				−1,200		
(7)	$4,300 +	$300 +	$2,000	=	$800	+	$5,800

Transaction (8) After taking an inventory at the end of the month, Mark Himes found
March 31   **that he had used $200 worth of supplies.** The original amount of supplies purchased has been reduced to the amount that was found to be left at the end of the month. Therefore, the difference was the amount used ($300 − $100 = $200). This reduces the asset Supplies by $200 and reduces capital by the same amount. It is termed *supplies expense*.

	Assets			=	Liabilities	+	Capital
	Cash +	Supplies +	Furniture		Accounts Payable		Mark Himes, Capital
	$4,300	$300	$2,000		$800		$5,800
		−200					−200 Supplies Expense
(8)	$4,300 +	$100 +	$2,000	=	$800	+	$5,600

Transaction (9) Withdraw $400 for personal use. The withdrawal of cash is a reduction
March 31   not only in Mark Himes's cash position but also in his capital. This is *not an expense* but a personal withdrawal, a reduction of the amount invested.

	Assets			=	Liabilities	+	Capital
	Cash +	Supplies +	Furniture		Accounts Payable		Mark Himes, Capital
	$4,300	$100	$2,000		$800		$5,600
	−400						−400 Drawing
(9)	$3,900 +	$100 +	$2,000	=	$800	+	$5,200

Chapter 1 The Fundamental Accounting Concepts and Principles（会计概述） 27

Mark Himes, Attorney
Month of March, 200X

	Assets				=	Liabilities	+	Capital
	Cash	+	Supplies	+ Furniture		Accounts Payable		Mark Himes, Capital
(1)	$4,000							$4,000
(2)	−300	+	$300					
	3,700	+	$300		=			$4,000
(3)				$2,000		$2,000		
	$3,700	+	$300	+ $2,000	=	$2,000		+$4,000
(4)	+2,500							+2,500 Fees Income
	$6,200	+	$300	+ $2,000	=	$2,000		+$6,500
(5)	−500							−500 Rent Expense
	$5,700	+	$300	+ $2,000	=	$2,000		+$6,000
(6)	−200							−200 Salaries Expense
	$5,500	+	$300	+ $2,000	=	$2,000		+$5,800
(7)	−1,200					−$1,200		
	$4,300	+	$300	+ $2,000	=	$800		+$5,800
(8)	−200							−200 Supplies Expense
	$4,300	+	$100	+ $2,000	=	$800		+$5,600
(9)	−400							−400 Drawing
	$3,900	+	$100	+ $2,000	=	$800		+$5,200

 New Words, Phrases and Special Terms

account payable   应付账款，应付未付账
accounts receivable   应收账款
asset   n.   资产

balance sheet		资产负债表
equation	n.	等式
capital	n.	资本
claim	n.	（根据权利提出）要求，主张
creditor	n.	债权人
due from		应收
exceed	vt.	超越
equity	n.	权益
expense	n.	费用
fees income		规费收入
financial position		财务地位（状况）
fundamental	adj.	基础的，基本的
government bond		政府公债
incur	vt.	承受，承担
liability	n.	负债
merchandise	n.	商品，货物
net income		纯收益，净收入，收益净额
net loss		净损失
notes payable		应付票据
owe	vt.	欠（债等）
owner	n.	业主，所有人
owner's equity		所有者权益，业主权益
patent right		专利权
property	n.	所有物，财产
reconcile	vt.	使……一致
render	vt.	提供
rent	n.	租金，房租
rent expense		租赁费
revenue	n.	收入
salaries expense		薪金
supplies expense		物料用品费
the accounting equation		会计等式
transaction	n.	交易，业务
variation	n.	变化，变异
withdraw	vt.	取（款），提款

withdrawal　　　　　n.　　　　　　　　　撤资，取款

 Notes

1. The three basic accounting elements are assets, liabilities and capital. They exist in every business entity.
会计三要素是资产、负债和资本，这三要素存在于任何一个企业主体。

2. The financial condition or position of a business enterprise is represented by the relationship of assets to liabilities and capital.
一个企业的财务状况是由资产对负债和资本的关系来表示的。

3. These three basic elements are connected by a fundamental relationship called balance sheet equation, sometimes called simply the accounting equation.
资产、负债和资本这三个基本要素之间有一个基本关系，这一关系叫做资产负债表等式，或简称为会计恒等式。

会计恒等式是企业财务状况的表达式。企业取得和持有的资产非来自业主投资，即来自信贷，如赊购货物（purchase on credit）、向银行借款（bank loan）或发行债券（issuances of bonds）等。因此，在任何时刻，某一企业的资产恒等于其业主和债权人对这些资产的要求权。其中，债权人的要求权总是优先于业主的要求权，因为企业必须承担如期偿还债务的责任。

4. This equation expresses the equality of the assets on one side with the claims of the creditors and owners on the other side: Assets = Liabilities + Capital.
会计等式表示一定数额的资产必等于一定数额的权益（负债和资本），即：资产 = 负债 + 资本。

 Section II　Review & Exercises（复习与练习）

 Summary

1. _____ may be defined as a process of identifying, measuring and communicating economic information to permit informed judgments and decisions.

2. The accounting profession has developed standards that are generally accepted and universally practiced. This common set of standards is called _____.

3. The basic accounting equation is _____ = _____ + _____.

4. Items owned by a business that have money value are known as _____.

5. _____ is the interest of the owners in a business.

6. Money owed to an outsider is a _____.

7. The difference between assets and liabilities is _____.
8. An investment in the business increases _____ and _____.
9. To purchase "on account" is to create a _____.
10. When the word "paid" occurs, it means a deduction of _____.
11. Income increases net assets and also _____.
12. A withdrawal of cash reduces cash and _____.
13. As each _____ is recorded, the accounting elements are affected.
14. At all times the accounting equation must be _____.
15. The five major account classifications are Assets, Liabilities, Capital (Owners' Equity), _____, and _____.

Questions

1. What is the purpose of accounting?
2. How do the functions of private accountants and public accountants differ?
3. Explain why accounting is a necessitated information system in modern business.
4. State the most fundamental concepts underlying the accounting process.
5. By whom are "generally accepted accounting principles" formulated in U.S.A.?

Solved Problems

1. Indicate whether each of the following is identified with (1) an asset, (2) a liability, or (3) capital.
   (a) fees earned
   (b) supplies
   (c) wages expense
   (d) land
   (e) accounts payable
   (f) cash
   (g) owners' investment
   (h) equipment

2. Determine the missing amount for each of the following:

	Assets	=	Liabilities	+	Capital
(1)	X	=	$20,000	+	$31,500
(2)	$62,750	=	X	+	10,000
(3)	57,000	=	38,000	+	X

(4)　　X　　=　　4,280　　+　　8,420
(5)　18,000　=　　X　　+　6,000
(6)　20,000　=　5,600　+　　X

3. Determine the effect of the following transactions on capital.
(1) Bought machinery on account.
(2) Paid the above bill.
(3) Withdrew money for personal use.
(4) Received fees for services rendered.
(5) Bought supplies for cash.
(6) Inventory of supplies decreased by the end of the month.

4. If total assets increased $20,000 during a period and total liabilities increased $12,000 during the same period. Determine the amount and direction (increase or decrease) of the change in owner's equity for that period.

5. Determine the net effect of the transactions listed below, using I = increase; D = decrease; NE = no effect.
(1) Invested cash in a business.
(2) Purchased equipment for cash.
(3) Purchased supplies on account.
(4) Paid creditors.
(5) Borrowed $5,000 from bank.
(6) Received fees.
(7) Withdrew money for personal use.

Assets	=	Liabilities	+	Capital
(1)				
(2)				
(3)				
(4)				
(5)				
(6)				
(7)				

6. T. Drew invests in his new firm $8,600 cash, $4,000 worth of supplies, equipment, and machinery valued at $12,000, and a $5,000 note payable based on the equipment and machinery. What is the capital of the firm?

7. Record the following entry: Bought an automobile for $14,000, paying $3,000 cash and giving a note for the balance.

	Assets	=	Liabilities	+ Capital
	Cash Equipment		Notes Payable	
Balance	$15,000			$15,000
Entry(?)	_____		_____	_____
Balance(?)				

8. Record the following entry: The inventory of supplies at the end of the year is valued at $2,200.

	Assets	=	Liabilities	+	Capital
	Supplies				
Balance (Beginning of month)	$6,400	=		+	$6,400
Entry(?)	_____				_____
Balance(?) (End of month)					

9. The total assets and total liabilities of Coca-Cola and PepsiCo at the end of their 1999 fiscal years are shown below.

	Coca-Cola (in millions)	PepsiCo (in millions)
Assets	$21,623	$17,551
Liabilities	$12,110	$10,670

Determine the owner's equity of each company.

10. The summary data of the Ellery's laundry are presented below. Describe each transaction.

```
              Assets              =  Liabilities    +  Capital
        Cash  + Supplies + Machinery = Accounts Payable
(1) $8,000   + $4,000   + $5,000                + $17,000
(2) – 3,000  +  3,000
(3) – 2,000              +9,000        +7,000
(4) + 9,000                                     + 9,000 Laundry Income
(5) – 1,200                                     – 1,200 Salaries Expense
```

(6) – 2,000   – 2,000 Supplies Expense
(7) – 7,000   –7,000
(8) – 1,000   –1,000 Withdrawal
     $2,800 $5,000 $14,000   =   —   +$21,800

11．Summary financial data of the Rag Time Band Co. For October are presented below in transaction form.

(1) Began operations by depositing $22,000 in a business bank account.

(2) Purchased musical equipment for $10,000, paying $4,000 in cash with the balance on account.

(3) Purchased supplies for cash, $500.

(4) Cash income received for musical engagement, $3,000.

(5) Paid salaries for the month, $1,200.

(6) Paid general expenses, $600.

(7) Paid $1,000 on account (see transaction 2).

(8) The inventory of supplies on hand at the end of the month was $200.

Record the transactions and running balances below.

	Assets			=	Liabilities	+	Capital
	Cash	Supplies	Equipment		Accounts Payable		Rag Time Band Co.
(1)							
(2)	___	___	___		___		___
Balance				=			
(3)	___	___	___		___		___
Balance				=			
(4)	___	___	___		___		___
Balance				=			
(5)	___	___	___		___		___
Balance				=			
(6)	___	___	___		___		___
Balance				=			
(7)	___	___	___		___		___
Balance				=			
(8)	___	___	___		___		___
Balance	___	___	___	=	___		___

12．Robert Lawn has just passed the law exam and started practicing. Below are his first month's transactions.

Jan. 1 Began business by investing $5,000 cash and land with a valne of $4,500.
    4 Purchased $750 worth of supplies on account.
    9 Paid rent for the month, $300.
    15 Received $1,100 for legal fees.
    17 Paid salaries for month, $1,900.
    21 Purchased printing equipment for $1,000 cash.
    24 Paid $500 on account.
    27 Withdrew $500 for personal expenses.
    29 Made improvements to land, paying $1,500 cash.
    31 Supplies on hand, $400.

Record the transactions and running balances in the form below.

	Assets	=	Liabilities	+	Capital
	Cash + Supplies + Equipment+Land		Accounts Payable		R. Lawn
Jan. 1	___ ___ ___ ___		___		___
4	___ ___ ___ ___		___		___
Balance	___ ___ ___ ___	=	___		___
9	___ ___ ___ ___		___		___
Balance	___ ___ ___ ___	=	___		___
15	___ ___ ___ ___		___		___
Balance	___ ___ ___ ___	=	___		___
17	___ ___ ___ ___		___		___
Balance	___ ___ ___ ___	=	___		___
21	___ ___ ___ ___		___		___
Balance	___ ___ ___ ___	=	___		___
24	___ ___ ___ ___		___		___
Balance	___ ___ ___ ___	=	___		___
27	___ ___ ___ ___		___		___
Balance	___ ___ ___ ___	=	___		___
29	___ ___ ___ ___		___		___
Balance	___ ___ ___ ___	=	___		___
31	___ ___ ___ ___		___		___
Balance	___ ___ ___ ___	=	___		___

13．Financial information of B. Glatt, Carpenter, for December is presented below.

(1) Began business by investing $14,000 cash and $6,000 equipment in the business.

(2) Bought additional equipment for $2,000 on account.
(3) Purchased supplies, $600, for cash.
(4) Paid $500 to creditor on account.
(5) Received $2,400 in fees earned during the month.
(6) Paid salary of part-time assistant, $300.
(7) Paid general expenses, $400.
(8) Paid balance due on equipment.
(9) Withdrew $700 for personal use.
(10) Cost of supplies used during month, $450.

Enter each transaction in the form below.

	Assets			=	Liabilities	+	Capital
	Cash	+ Supplies	+ Equipment		Accounts Payable		B. Glatt, Capital
(1)							
(2)	____	____	____		____		____
Balance				=			
(3)	____	____	____		____		____
Balance				=			
(4)	____	____	____		____		____
Balance				=			
(5)	____	____	____		____		____
Balance				=			
(6)	____	____	____		____		____
Balance				=			
(7)	____	____	____		____		____
Balance				=			
(8)	____	____	____		____		____
Balance				=			
(9)	____	____	____		____		____
Balance				=			
(10)	____	____	____		____		____
Balance	____	____	____	=	____		____

14. M. Boyd operates a taxi company known as the Boyd Taxi Co. The balances of his accounts as of July 1 of the current year are as follows: cash, $6,400; supplies, $800; automobile, $4,500; accounts payable, $2,000; capital, $9,700. The transactions of the firm during the month of July appear below.

(1) Paid the balance owed to the creditor.
(2) Income (cash) for the month, $8,200.
(3) Paid wages for the month, $1,900.
(4) Paid for advertising, $200.
(5) Purchased an additional used taxi for $5,000, terms half in cash and the balance on account.
(6) Paid $425 for maintenance of automobiles.
(7) Sold $100 of our supplies at cost as an accommodation.
(8) Withdrew $800 for personal use.
(9) Inventory of supplies at the end of the month was $350.
Enter each transaction in the form below.

	Assets			=	Liabilities	+	Capital
	Cash	+ Supplies	+ Automobiles		Accounts Payable		Capital
Balance	$6,400	$800	$4,500		$2,000		$9,700
(1)	____	____	____		____		____
Balance				=			
(2)	____	____	____		____		____
Balance				=			
(3)	____	____	____		____		____
Balance				=			
(4)	____	____	____		____		____
Balance				=			
(5)	____	____	____		____		____
Balance				=			
(6)	____	____	____		____		____
Balance				=			
(7)	____	____	____		____		____
Balance				=			
(8)	____	____	____		____		____
Balance				=			
(9)	____	____	____		____		____
Balance	____	____	____	=	____		____

Section III Reading Material（阅读材料）

The Assets Section of Balance Sheet

There are three basis *financial statements*（财务报表）which are the end products of financial accounting: *Balance Sheet*（资产负债表）, *Income Statement*（损益表）and the *Statement of Cash Flows*（现金流量表）. Balance sheet and income statement are prepared at least yearly, but it is also customary to prepare them quarterly or monthly.

Balance Sheet is a listing of an organization's assets, liabilities and owners' equity on a given date. It is designed to *portray*（说明）the financial position of the organization at a particular time (e.g., on January 31, 2000). As presented in Exhibit 1-1, the three major sections of the balance sheet are presented in the T-account format. This presentation allows the users to tell at a glance that total assets (e.g., $259,000) are being financed by two sources: $79,000 by the creditors (i.e., liabilities) and $180,000 by the owner (i.e., owners' equity). An important aspect of this statement is that the total assets always equal to the sum of liabilities and owners' equity. This balancing is sometimes described as the accounting equation: Assets = Liabilities + Owners' Equity.

Assets are the economic resources of an organization that can usefully be expressed in monetary terms. The assets of Douglas Company have further classified into *current assets*（流动资产）and *long-term assets*（长期资产）. Current assets are cash and the assets that will be converted into cash or used up during the *normal operating cycle*（正常经营周期）of the business or one year, whichever is longer. Current assets are usually listed in the order of their "*liquidity*（变现能力）" or *convertibility*（可兑换性）into cash. Some examples of current assets *other than*（除了）those shown in Exhibit 1-1 are notes receivable and *marketable securities*（有价证券）. *Prepaid expenses*（预付费用）such as insurance, rent, and supplies are normally consumed during the operating cycle rather than converted into cash.

Exhibit 1-1

DOUGLAS TRADING COMPANY
Balance Sheet
January 31, 2000

Assets		Liabilities and Owners' Equity	
Current Assets		Current Liabilities	
Cash	$65,000	Notes Payable	$16,000
Accounts Receivable	34,000	Accounts Payable	59,000

Inventory	98,000	Accrued Salaries Payable	4,000
Prepaid Insurance	3,500	Total Current Liabilities	$79,000
Supplies on hand	1,500		
Total Current Assets	$202,000		
Fixed Assets		Owners' Equity	
Store Fixtures	$72,000	K. Douglas, Capital	$180,000
Less: Accumulated Depreciation 15,000	$57,000	Total Liabilities and	
Total Assets	$259,000	Owners' Equity	$259,000

Long-term assets are relatively long-lived assets used in operating an organization and may be further classified into *fixed assets*（固定资产）（or plant and equipment）and *intangible assets*（无形资产）. Fixed assets may include land, buildings, and various kinds of equipment（machinery, *store fixtures*（店面装置）, office equipment, delivery equipment, etc.）. They constitute the major category of the long term assets. *Depreciable assets*（应折旧资产）are normally shown at their *original cost*（原始成本）. The accumulated portion of the cost taken as depreciation to date is subtracted from its original cost to obtain the *book value*（账面价值）of the asset. Intangible assets are characterized by the legal claims or rights which may include *patents*（专利权）, *trademarks*（商标）, *franchises*（特许经营权）, *goodwill*（商誉）, etc.

 Answer the following questions:

(1) What is the purpose of a balance sheet?
(2) What is the important aspect of a balance sheet?
(3) Define "assets".
(4) Define "current assets" and "long-term assets".
(5) List at least six examples of current assets and three examples of long-term assets.

Chapter 2 Debits and Credits: The Double-Entry System

（借方和贷方：复式记账法）

导学： 复式记账（double-entry accounting）是指对于发生的每一项经济业务，都要以相等的金额，在相互联系的两个或两个以上的账户中进行登记的一种记账方法。在会计核算中，为了能够记录和反映经济业务引起的资金量的增减变动情况，我们设置了会计科目（chart of accounts）和账户（accounts）。所谓会计科目，就是根据会计要素，按其不同的具体内容进行归类的项目名称。账户是根据会计科目的名称开设、用来专门记录和反映企业经济业务变动情况及其变动结果的户头。为了更好地使用和了解账户，我们可以对账户分类（ledger）。试算平衡表（a trial balance）通过检查借方余额与贷方余额合计是否相等来检验会计处理的准确性。

 Section I Accounting Study（会计学习）

2.1 The Account
（账户）

Usefulness of an Account

Before making a major cash purchase, such as buying a CD player, you need to know the balance of your bank account. Likewise, managers need timely, useful information in order to make good decisions about their businesses.

How are accounting systems designed to provide this information? We illustrated a very simple design in Chapter 1, where transactions were recorded and summarized in the accounting equation format. However, preparing a new equation $A = L + C$ after each transaction would be cumbersome and costly, especially when there are a great many transactions in an accounting period. Also, information for a specific item such as cash would be lost as successive transactions were recorded. This information could be obtained by going back and summarizing the transactions, but that would be very time-consuming. Thus we begin with the account.

Characteristics of an Account

An *account* may be defined as *a record of the increases, decreases, and balances in an individual item of asset, liability, capital, income (revenue), or expense.*

An account, in its simplest form, has three parts. First, each account has a title, which is the name of the item recorded in the account. Second, each account has a space for recording increases in the amount of the item. Third, each account has a space for recording decreases in the amount of the item. The simplest form of the account is known as the ***T account***, because it resembles the letter T. The left side of the account is called the debit side, and the right side of the account is called the credit side.

Title	
Left side	Right side
debit	*credit*

When an amount is entered on the left side of an account, it is a ***debit***, and the account is said to be ***debited*** (or charged). When an amount is entered on the right side, it is a ***credit***, and the account is said to be ***credited***. Debits and credits are sometimes abbreviated as ***Dr.*** and ***Cr.***.

Example 1

Cash	
700	600
400	200
600	*800*
900 *1,700*	

Note that the left side of the account adds up to $1,700, while the right side totals $800. The $1,700 and $800 totals, respectively, are written in smaller type and are known as footings. The difference between the total amounts is $900 and is called the ending balance. Since the larger total $1,700 appears on the left side of the account, the ending balance of $900 is placed there. Had the right side total been greater than the left, the ending balance would have appeared on the right side.

Example 2

In the cash account that follows, transactions involving receipts of cash are listed on the debit side of the account. The transactions involving cash payments are listed on the credit side. If at any time the total of the cash receipts is needed, the entries on the debit side of the account may be added and the total ($10,950) inserted below the last debit. Remember that the amount, called a memorandum balance, should be written in small figures or identified in some other way to avoid mistaking the amount for an additional debit. The total of the cash payments, $6,850 in the example, may be inserted on the credit side in a similar manner. Subtracting the smaller sum from the larger, $10,950 – $6,850, identifies the amount of cash on hand, $4,100. This amount is called the **balance of the account**. It may be inserted in the account, next to the total of the debit column. In this way, the balance is identified as a **debit balance**. If a balance sheet were to be prepared at this time, cash of $4,100 would be reported.

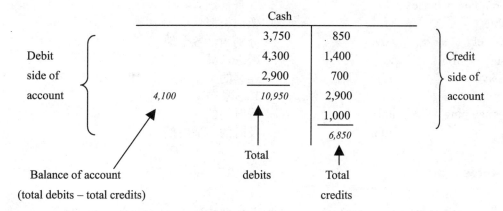

New Words, Phrases and Special Terms

abbreviate	v.	简写成，缩写为
account	n.	账户
balance	n.	余额
bank account		银行账户
cash account		现金账户
cash on hand		库存现金
cash purchase		现金购买
charge	vt.	借记，收费
credit	n.	贷方，贷记
credit side		贷方
cumbersome	adj.	笨重的，麻烦的
debit	n.	借方，借记
debit balance		借方余额

debit side		借方
difference	n.	[数]差额
double-entry system		复式记账法
ending balance		最终余额
footing	n.	合计，结算总额
identify	vt.	识别，鉴别
insert	vt.	插入，嵌入
likewise	adv.	同样地
memorandum	n.	备忘录
memorandum balance		备查余额
resemble	vt.	像，类似
respectively	adv.	分别地，各个地
subtract(～ from)	v.	减去，减
successive	adj.	连续的
T account	n.	T 形账户
time-consuming	adj.	费时间的
timely	adj.	及时的，适时的

 Notes

1. The simplest form of the account is known as the ***T account***, because it resembles the letter T.
最简单的账户形式被称为 **T 形账户**，因为它的形状像字母 T。

2. The left side of the account is called the debit side, and the right side of the account is called the credit side.
T 形账户的左边称为借方，右边称为贷方。

3. When an amount is entered on the left side of an account, it is a ***debit***, and the account is said to be debited (or charged). When an amount is entered on the right side, it is a ***credit***, and the account is said to be credited. Debits and credits are sometimes abbreviated as Dr. and Cr..
一个数额记在账户的左边，就是借方记录，这个账户就是被借记。当一个数额记在账户的右边，那就是贷方记录，这个账户就是被贷记。借贷两个字常被缩写为 Dr.和 Cr.。

4. ending balance 期末余额，包括期末借方余额（ending debit balance，借方大于贷方）和贷方余额（ending credit balance，贷方大于借方）。资产和费用类账户通常有期末借方余额。

2.2 The Rules of Debit and Credit
（借贷记账规则）

In Chapter 1, we saw how business transactions cause a change in one or more of the three basic accounting elements. Accuracy is improved because the accounting equation must balance after each transaction. The equality of debits and credits provides the basis for the universally used double-entry system of recording transactions. Luca Pacioli, an Italian monk, introduced double-entry accounting back in 1494. The reason that double-entry accounting has been in existence for over 500 years is because it ensures accuracy.

Learning the rules of debits and credits is similar to learning the rules on how to drive a car. You learn to drive your car on the right side of the road. As you learn debits and credits, remember there are established rules that everyone must follow. The following tables summarize the rules of debit and credit.

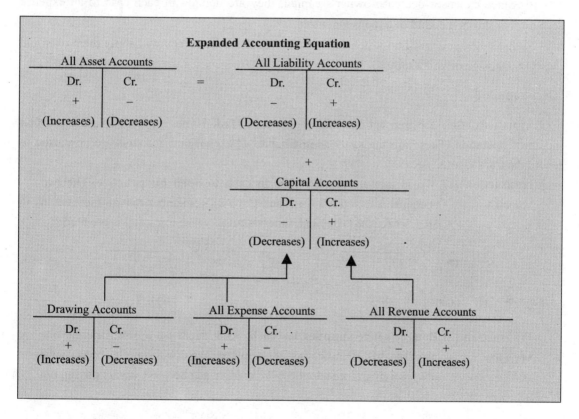

As described in these T accounts, the rules for recording transactions under a double-entry system may be expressed as follows:

(1) Increases in assets are debited to asset accounts; therefore, decreases must be credited.

(2) Increases in liability and capital items are credited to liability and capital accounts;

therefore, decreases must be debited.

Capital was increased by the owner's investments and by revenues. Capital was decreased by expenses and by withdrawals. With this recollection, we offer these additional rules:

(3) Investments by the owner of a business are credited to the owner's capital account.

(4) Since the owner's withdrawals of assets decrease owner's capital, they are debited to the owner's drawing account.

(5) Since revenues increase capital, they are credited in each case to a revenue account that shows the kind of revenue earned.

(6) Since expenses decrease owner's capital, they are debited in each case to an expense account that shows the kind of expense incurred.

At this stage, you will find it helpful to memorize these rules. You will apply them over and over in the course of your study.

Example 3

Let us reexamine the transactions that occurred in Mark Himes's practice during the first month of operation. These are the same as in Chapter 1, except that accounts are now used to record the transactions.

Transaction (1) Mr. Himes invested $4,000 in cash to open his practice. The two accounts affected are Cash and Capital. Remember that an increase in an asset (cash) is debited, whereas an increase in capital is credited.

March 1

Cash		Capital	
Dr.	Cr.	Dr.	Cr.
+	−	−	+
(1) 4,000			4,000 (1)

Transaction (2) Bought office supplies for cash, $300. Here we are substituting one asset (cash) for another asset (supplies). We debit Supplies because we are receiving more supplies. We credit Cash because we are paying out cash.

March 4

Cash		Supplies	
Dr.	Cr.	Dr.	Cr.
+	−	+	−
4,000	300 (2)	(2) 300	

Chapter 2 Debits and Credits: The Double-Entry System（借方和贷方：复式记账法）

Transaction (3) **Bought office furniture from Stanley Furniture Company on account, $2,000.** We are receiving an asset and, therefore, debit Furniture to show the increase. We are not paying cash but creating a new liability, thereby increasing the liability account (Accounts Payable).

March 5

Furniture		Accounts Payable	
Dr.	Cr.	Dr.	Cr.
+	−	−	+
(3) 2,000			2,000 (3)

Transaction (4) **Received $2,500 in fees earned during the month.** In this case, we are increasing the asset account Cash, since we have received $2,500. Therefore, we debit it. We are increasing the capital, yet we do not credit Capital. It is better temporarily to separate the income from the owners' equity (capital) and create a new account, Fees Income (also known as Revenue) .

March 15

Cash		Fees Income	
Dr.	Cr.	Dr.	Cr.
+	−	−	+
4,000	300		2,500 (4)
(4) 2,500			

Transaction (5) **Paid office rent for March, $500.** We must decrease the asset account Cash because we are paying out money. Therefore, we credit it. It is preferable to keep expenses separated from the owners' equity. Therefore, we open a new account for the expense involved, Rent Expense . The $500 is entered on the left side, since expense decreases capital.

March 30

Cash		Rent Expense	
Dr.	Cr.	Dr.	Cr.
+	−	+	−
4,000	300	(5) 500	
2,500	500 (5)		

Transaction (6) **Paid salary for part-time help, $200.** Again, we must reduce our asset account Cash because we are paying out money. Therefore, we credit

March 30

the account. Himes' Capital was reduced by an expense; thus we open another account, Salaries Expense. A debit to this account shows the decrease in capital.

Cash		Salaries Expense	
Dr.	Cr.	Dr.	Cr.
+	−	+	−
4,000	300	(6) 200	
2,500	500		
	200 (6)		

Transaction (7) **Paid $1,200 to Stanley Furniture Company on account.** This
March 31 transaction reduced our asset Cash because we are paying out money. We therefore credit Cash. We also reduce our liability Accounts Payable by $1,200; we now owe that much less. Thus, we debit Accounts Payable.

Cash		Salaries Expense	
Dr.	Cr.	Dr.	Cr.
+	−	−	+
4,000	300	(7) 1,200	2,000
2,500	500		
	200		
	1,200 (7)		

Transaction (8) **After taking an inventory at the end of the month, Himes found**
March 31 **that he had used $200 worth of supplies.** We must reduce the asset account supplies by crediting it for $200. Supplies Expense is debited for the decrease in capital. This is computed as follows: Beginning inventory of $300, less supplies on hand at the end of the month $100, indicates that $200 must have been used during the month.

Supplies		Supplies Expense	
Dr.	Cr.	Dr.	Cr.
+	−	+	−
300	200 (8)	(8) 200	

Transaction (9) **Withdraw $400 for personal use.** The withdrawal of cash means that
March 31 there is a reduction in the asset account Cash. Therefore, it is credited.

The amount invested by the owner is also $400 less. We must open the account Drawing, which is debited to show the decrease in capital.

	Cash			Drawing	
Dr.	Cr.			Dr.	Cr.
+	−			+	−
4,000	300		(9)	400	
2,500	500				
	200				
	1,200				
	400 (9)				

Normal Balance of Accounts

An account has a debit balance when the sum of its debits exceeds the sum of its credits; it has a credit balance when the sum of the credits is the greater. In ***double-entry accounting***, which is in almost universal use, there are equal debit and credit entries for every transaction. Where only two accounts are affected, the debit and credit amounts are equal. If more than two accounts are affected, the total of the debit entries must equal the total of the credit entries.

 New Words, Phrases and Special Terms

appropriate	adj.	适当的
balance of accounts		账户余额
basis	n.	基础
be credited to		把……记入贷方，贷记
be debited to		把……记入借方，借记
cash on hand		库存现金
category	n.	种类
compute	v.	计算
credit balance		贷方余额
credit entry		贷方分录
debit balance		借方余额
debit entry		借方分录
double-entry accounting		复式记账法
dual	adj.	双的，二重的
effect	n.	结果，效果

exceed	vt.	超越，胜过
equality	n.	相等
fees income (fees revenue)		规费收入
inventory	n.	存货，盘存，财产清册
monk	n.	修道士
preferable	adj.	更可取的，更好的
reexamine	vt.	复查
taking an inventory		盘存
recollection	n.	回忆，记忆，回想
thereby	adv.	因此，从而

 Notes

1. The equality of debits and credits provides the basis for the universally used double-entry system of recording transactions.

复式记账法被广泛应用于经济交易的记录，而借贷相等是复式记账法的基础。

2. Increases in assets are debited to asset accounts; therefore, decreases must be credited.

资产的增加记录在资产账户的借方，资产的减少记录在贷方。

3. Increases in liability and capital items are credited to liability and capital accounts; therefore, decreases must be debited.

负债和资本的增加记录在负债和资本账户的贷方，负债和资本的减少记录在借方。

4. An account has a debit balance when the sum of its debits exceeds the sum of its credits; it has a credit balance when the sum of the credits is the greater. In double-entry accounting, which is in almost universal use, there are equal debit and credit entries for every transaction. Where only two accounts are affected, the debit and credit amounts are equal. If more than two accounts are affected, the total of the debit entries must equal the total of the credit entries.

当一个账户上借项数超过贷项数时，这个账户就出现了借方余额；但当它的贷项数大于借项数时，则出现了贷方余额。在几乎全世界普遍使用的复式记账法下，每笔交易的借方和贷方数额相等。在只有两个账户受影响时，借贷双方的数额相等。但如果涉及两个以上的账户，那么记入借方的总数和记入贷方的总数必须相等。

5. Double-entry system: a system for recording transactions based on recording increases and decreases in accounts so that debits always equal credits.

复式记账法，亦称复式记账原理。由意大利著名数学家卢卡•帕乔利首次提出。西方现代会计理论正是在此基础上逐步发展起来的。复式记账是指对于发生的每一项经济业务，都要以相等的金额，在相互联系的两个或两个以上的账户中进行登记的一种记账方法。

6. taking an inventory　盘存。在定期盘存制下，盘存应于期末进行，并据此确定销售成本。为了对存货进行有效的管理，每年至少应对存货盘点一次，以核对存货的账面余额。

2.3　The Ledger and the Chart of Account
（会计分类账与会计科目表）

The Ledger

The complete set of accounts for a business entry is called a ***ledger***. It is the "reference book" of the accounting system and is used to classify and summarize transactions and to prepare data for financial statements. It is also a valuable source of information for managerial purposes, giving, for example, the amount of sales for the period or the cash balance at the end of the period.

Companies may use various kinds of ledgers, but every company has a general ledger. A general ledger contains all the assets, liabilities, and capital accounts. Whenever the term ledger is used in this textbook without a modifying adjective, it will mean the general ledger. The ledger provides a means of accumulating in one place all the information about changes in specific account balances.

The T-account form of an account is often very useful for illustration and analysis purposes because T accounts can be drawn so quickly. However, in practice, the account forms are much more structured. A form widely used in a manual system is illustrated below, using assumed data from the cash account of a certain company.

Cash　No. 10

Date	Explanation	Ref.	Dr.	Cr.	Balance
200X					
Dec. 2			20 000		20 000
4				6 000	14 000
5			3 200		17 200
11			6 000		23 200
17				10 200	13 000
23				350	12 650
30				7 500	5 150

The Chart of Accounts

It is desirable to establish a systematic method of identifying and locating each account in the ledger. The ***chart of accounts***, sometimes called the ***code of accounts***, is a listing of the accounts by title and numerical designation. In some companies, the chart of accounts may run to hundreds of items.

In designing a numbering structure for the accounts, it is important to provide adequate flexibility to permit expansion without having to revise the basic system. Generally, blocks of numbers are assigned to various groups of accounts, such as assets, liabilities, and so on. There are various systems of coding, depending on the needs and desires of the company.

A simple chart structure is to have the first digit represent the major group in which the account is located. Thus, accounts that have numbers beginning with 1 are assets; 2, liabilities; 3, capital; 4, income; and 5, expenses. The second or third digit designates the position of the account in the group.

In the two-digit system, assets are assigned the block of numbers 11~19, and liabilities 21~29. In larger firms, a three-digit (or higher) system may be used, with assets assigned 101~199 and liabilities 201~299. Following are the numerical designations for the account groups under both methods.

Account Group	Two-Digit	Three-Digit
1. Assets	11~19	101~199
2. Liabilities	21~29	201~299
3. Capital	31~39	301~399
4. Income	41~49	401~499
5. Expenses	51~59	501~599

Thus, Cash may be account 11 under the first system and 101 under the second system. The cash account may be further broken down as: 101, Cash—First National Bank; 102, Cash—Second National Bank; and so on.

Example 4

In this section, we will be explaining the accounting for the solo-proprietorship, Adams Graphic Design & Advertising Agency (a service enterprise). Accounts 1~19 indicate an asset account is involved; 20~29 indicate liabilities; 30~39 indicate capital accounts; 40~49, revenues; and 50~59, expenses. A partial chart of accounts for Adams Graphic Design & Advertising Agency (David Adams, owner) identifying some of its accounts is as follows:

Adams Graphic Design & Advertising Agency

Assets	Capital
1. Cash	30. David Adams, Capital
6. Fees Receivable	31. David Adams, Drawing
8. Advertising Supplies	**Revenues**
10. Prepaid Insurance	41. Fee Earned
15. Office Equipment	
Liabilities	**Expenses**
25. Notes payable	50. Salaries Expense
26. Accounts Payable	51. Advertising Supplies Expense
28. Unearned Fees	52. Rent Expense
	53. Insurance Expense

 New Words, Phrases and Special Terms

advertising	adj.	广告的
agency	n.	代理处，代理
assign	vt.	分配，指派
block	n.	（一）批
break down		分解
chart of accounts		会计科目表，账户一览表
classify	vt.	分类，分等
code of accounts		会计编码，账簿编号
designation	n.	指示，指定，名称
general ledger		总分类账
graphic	adj.	绘画的，图形的
ledger	n.	分类账
modifying adjective		修饰性形容词
numerical	adj.	数字的，用数表示的
reference book		参考书
run	vi.	蔓延，进行
proprietorship	n.	所有权
solo-proprietorship	n.	独资企业
summarize	vt.	概述，总结

systematic	adj.	系统的，体系的
the amount of sales		销售额

 Notes

1. The complete set of accounts for a business entry is called a ledger.

分类账是一个企业中记录业务往来的所有会记账户的集体名称。

2. The chart of accounts, sometimes called the code of accounts, is a listing of the accounts by title and numerical designation.

会计科目表，也称为账簿编码，是总分类账中所有账户的名称和编号的一览表。

3. In designing a numbering structure for the accounts, it is important to provide adequate flexibility to permit expansion without having to revise the basic system.

会计科目的编号设计要为未来会记账户的增加留有余地。这样，随着（企业）规模的扩展而不至于修改最基本的会记账户体系。

4. ledger （会计）分类账，是指明某项经济业务所涉及的应借、应贷的账户及其金额的记录。账户按资产、负债、所有者权益、收入、费用这五大类别的顺序排列成活页的账本。

5. chart of accounts 会计科目表，账户一览表。所谓会计科目，就是根据会计要素，按其不同的具体内容进行归类的项目名称。

2.4　The Trial Balance

（试算平衡表）

As every transaction results in an equal amount of debits and credits in the ledger, the total of all debit entries in the ledger should equal the total of all credit entries. At the end of the accounting period, we check this equality by preparing a two-column schedule called a ***trial balance***, which compares the total of all debit balances with the total of all credit balances. A trial balance may be defined as a list of all accounts with their balances—assets first, followed by liabilities and then capital. It provides a check on accuracy by showing whether the total debits equal the total credits. The procedure is as follows:

(1) List account titles in numerical order.

(2) Record balances of each account, entering debit balances in the left column and credit balances in the right column.

Note: Asset and expense accounts are debited for increases and normally would have debit balances. Liabilities, capital, and income accounts are credited for increases and normally would have credit balances.

(3) Add the columns and record the totals.

Chapter 2 Debits and Credits: The Double-Entry System（借方和贷方：复式记账法）

(4) Compare the totals. They must be the same.

If the totals agree, the trial balance is in balance, indicating that debits and credits are equal for the hundreds or thousands of transactions entered in the ledger. While the trial balance provides arithmetic proof of the accuracy of the records, it does not provide theoretical proof. For example, if the purchase of equipment was incorrectly charged to Expense, the trial balance columns may agree, but theoretically the accounts would be wrong, as Expense would be overstated and Equipment understated. In addition to providing proof of arithmetic accuracy in accounts, the trial balance facilitates the preparation of the periodic financial statements. Generally, the trial balance comprises the first two columns of a worksheet, from which financial statements are prepared.

Example 5

The summary of the transactions for Mr. Himes (see Example 3), and their effect on the accounts, is shown below. The trial balance is then taken.

Assets

Cash　　　　　11
(1)	4,000	300	(2)
(4)	2,500	500	(5)
3,900	6,500	200	(6)
		1,200	(7)
		400	(9)
		2,600	

Supplies　　　12
| (2) | 300 | 200 | (8) |
| | 100 | | |

Furniture　　　13
| (3) | 2,000 | | |

Liabilities

Accounts Payable　　21
| (7) | 1,200 | 2,000 | (3) |
| | | 800 | |

Capital

Capital　　　　31
| | | 4,000 | (1) |

Drawing　　　　32
| (9) | 400 | | |

Fees Income　　41
| | | 2,500 | (4) |

Rent Expense　　51
| (5) | 500 | | |

Salaries Expense　52
| (6) | 200 | | |

Supplies Expense 53
| (8) | 200 | | |

53

Mark Himes
Trial Balance
March 31, 200X

	Dr.	Cr.
Cash	$3,900	
Supplies	100	
Furniture	2,000	
Accounts Payable		$ 800
T. Drew, Capital		4,000
Drawing	400	
Fees Income		2,500
Rent Expense	500	
Salaries Expense	200	
Supplies Expense	200	
	$7,300	$7,300

 New Words, Phrases and Special Terms

agree	vi.	与……一致
arithmetic	adj.	算术的，计算的
comprise	vt.	包含，由……组成
facilitate	vt.	（不以人作主语的）推动，促进，有助于
numerical	adj.	数字的，用数表示的
overstate	vt.	高估
periodic	adj.	周期的，定期的
procedure	n.	程序，手续
proof	n.	证据，试验
result in		导致
theoretical	adj.	理论的
trial balance		试算平衡表
two-column schedule		两栏式表格
understate	v.	低估
worksheet	n.	工作底表

Notes

1. A trial balance may be defined as a list of all accounts with their balances—assets first, followed by liabilities and then capital.

试算平衡表定义为列示所有账户余额的表式。该表式按资产、负债和资本（所有者权益）的顺序列示。

2. It provides a check on accuracy by showing whether the total debits equal the total credits.

试算平衡表通过检查借方与贷方余额是否相等，来检验会计处理的准确性。

3. 试算平衡表（trial balance）和工作底表（worksheet）都是实际会计工作编制的内部使用表式，并不对外报告。

Section II Review & Exercises（复习与练习）

Summary

1. To classify and summarize a single item of an account group, we use a form called an _____.
2. Every transaction affects at least two accounts. This forms the basis of _____.
3. The accounts make up a record called a _____.
4. The left side of the account is known as the _____, while the right side is the _____.
5. Increases in all asset accounts are _____.
6. Increases in all liability accounts are _____.
7. Increases in all capital accounts are _____.
8. Increases in all income accounts are _____.
9. Increases in all expense accounts are _____.
10. Expenses are debited because they decrease _____.
11. A _____ shows the ending balance for assets, liabilities, capital, revenue and expense accounts. The left-side column lists the debit balances and the right-side column lists the credit balances. Total debits must equal total credits.

Questions

1. What are the advantages of preparing an account?
2. List the characteristics of an account.
3. Describe the rules of debit and credit.
4. Distinguish the major differences between the ledger and the chart of accounts.

5. What are the major functions of preparing a trial balance

 Solved Problems

1. In each of the following types of T accounts, enter an increase (by writing +) and a decrease (by writing –).

```
      Assets              Liabilities            Capital
   Dr.  |  Cr.          Dr.  |  Cr.           Dr.  |  Cr.


      Income                                  Expense
   Dr.  |  Cr.                              Dr.  |  Cr.
```

2. Below is a list of accounts. Rearrange the accounts as they would appear in the ledger and assign a numerical designation for each one from these numbers: 17, 22, 32, 59, 12, 51, 41, 11, 21, and 31.

Accounts

Accounts Payable

Accounts Receivable

Capital

Cash

Drawing

Equipment

Fees Income

Miscellaneous Expense

Notes Payable

Rent Expense

3. Indicate in the column below the increases and decrease in each account by placing a check mark in the appropriate column.

		Debit	Credit
(1)	Capital is increased		
(2)	Cash is decreased		
(3)	Accounts Payable is increased		
(4)	Rent Expense is increased		
(5)	Equipment is increased		
(6)	Fees Income is increased		
(7)	Capital is decreased (through drawing)		

4. For each transaction in the table below, indicate the account to be debited and the account to be credited by placing the letter representing the account in the appropriate column.

Name of Account	Transaction	Dr.	Cr.
(1) Accounts Payable	1. Invested cash in the firm		
(2) Capital	2. Paid rent for month		
(3) Cash	3. Received cash fees for services		
(4) Drawing	4. Paid salaries		
(5) Equipment	5. Bought equipment on account		
(6) Fees Income	6. Paid balance on equipment		
(7) Notes Payable	7. Bought supplies on account		
(8) Rent Expense	8. Borrowed money from bank, giving a note in exchange		
(9) Salaries Expense	9. Supplies inventory showed one-third used during the month		
(10) Supplies			
(11) Supplies Expense	10. Withdrew cash for personal use		

5. Record each *separate transaction* in the accompanying accounts.

(1) Bought supplies on account for $600.

(2) Bought equipment for $2,700, paying one-third down and owing the balance.

(3) Gave a note in settlement of transaction (2).

(4) Received $500 in plumbing（水管安装）fees.

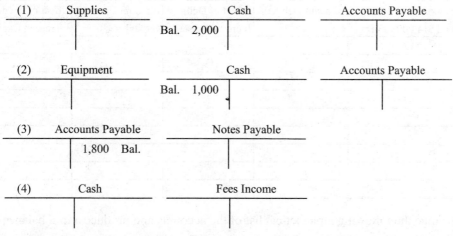

6. The ten accounts that follow summarize the first week's transactions of the A.B.C. Taxi Company.

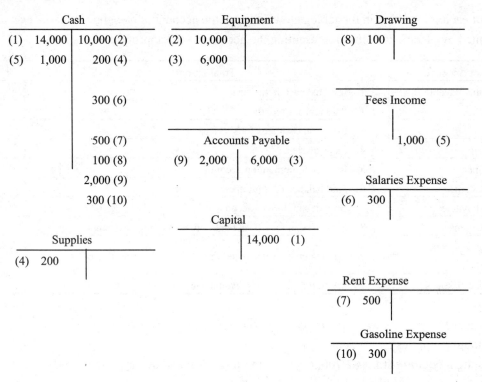

Complete the form below. (The analysis of the first transaction is given as a sample.)

	Transaction	Account Debited	Effect of Debit	Account Credited	Effect of Credit
(1)	Invested $14,000 in firm	Cash	Increased asset	Capital	Increased Capital
(2)					
(3)					
(4)					
(5)					
(6)					
(7)					
(8)					
(9)					
(10)					

7. Rearrange the following alphabetical list of the accounts and produce a trial balance.

Accounts Payable	9,000	General Expense	1,000
Accounts Receivable	14,000	Notes Payable	11,000
Capital, P. Henry	32,000	Rent Expense	5,000

Cash	20,000	Salaries Expense	8,000
Drawing, P. Henry	4,000	Supplies	6,000
Equipment	18,000	Supplies Expense	2,000
Fees Income	26,000		

8. The M. Ramirez Company's trial balance appears below. Certain accounts have been recorded improperly from the ledger to the trial balance, causing it not to balance. Present a corrected trial balance based on normal balances of each account.

M. Ramirez
Trial Balance
March 31, 200X

	Dr.	Cr.
Cash	$29,000	
Accounts Receivable		$ 4,000
Accounts Payable	3,000	
Capital		12,500
Drawing		500
Fees Income	33,000	
Rent Expense	1,000	
Salaries Expense	10,000	
General Expense		4,000
	$76,000	$21,000

9. The trial balance of P. Johnson does not balance as presented. In reviewing the ledger, you discover the following:

(1) The debits and credits in the cash account total $24,100 and $21,400, respectively.

(2) The $400 received in settlement of an account was not posted to the Accounts Receivable account.

(3) The balance of the Salaries Expense account should be $200 less.

(4) No balance should exist in the Notes Payable account.

(5) Each account should have a normal balance.

Prepare a corrected trial balance.

P. Johnson
Trial Balance
December 31, 200X

	Dr.	Cr.
Cash	$ 3,000	

Accounts Receivable	11,800	
Supplies		$800
Equipment	18,500	
Accounts Payable		1,500
Notes Payable		300
Johnson, Capital		15,400
Johnson, Drawing		500
Fees Income		29,000
Salaries Expense	8,200	
Rent Expense	3,000	
Supplies Expense		200
General Expense		800
	$44,500	$48,500

10. Using the information of Problem 1.13, record the entries in the accounts below for B. Glatt, labeling each item by number as in Problem 1.13. Then prepare a trial balance.

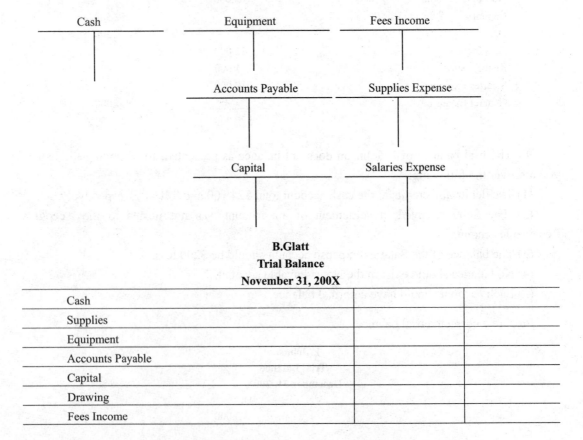

B.Glatt
Trial Balance
November 31, 200X

Cash		
Supplies		
Equipment		
Accounts Payable		
Capital		
Drawing		
Fees Income		

Rent Expense		
Salaries Expense		

Supplies   Drawing   General Expense

11. For each transaction below, record the entry in the T accounts furnished.

(1) The Nu-Look Dry Cleaning Company opened a business bank account by depositing $12,000 on Nov. 1.

(2) Purchased supplies for cash, $220.

(3) Purchased dry cleaning equipment for $3,500, paying $1,500 in cash with the balance on account.

(4) Paid rent for the month, $425.

(5) Cash sales for the month totaled $1,850.

(6) Paid salaries of $375.

(7) Paid $500 on account.

(8) The cost of supplies used was determined to be $60.

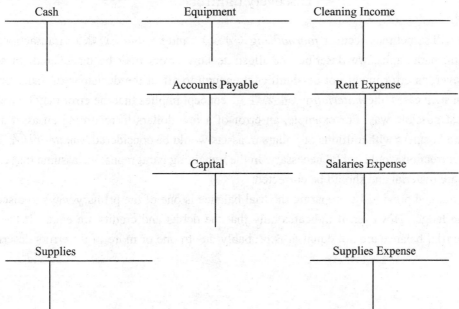

12. Prepare a trial balance as of November 30 for the Nu-Look Dry Cleaning Company, using the account balances in Problem 2.11.

Nu-Look Dry Cleaning Company
Trial Balance
November 30, 200X

Cash		
Supplies		
Equipment		
Accounts Payable		
Nu-Look Dry Cleaning Company, Capital		
Cleaning Income		
Rent Expense		
Salaries Expense		
Supplies Expense		

Section III   Reading Material（阅读材料）

Discovery of Errors

Errors will sometimes occur in *journalizing*（分录） and *posting*（过账） transactions. In the following paragraphs, we describe and illustrate how errors may be discovered. In some cases, however, an error might not be significant enough to affect the decisions of management or others. In such cases, the *materiality*（重要性） concept implies that the error may be treated in the easiest possible way. For example, an error of a few dollars in recording an asset as an expense for a business with millions of dollars in assets would be considered *immaterial*（不重要的）, and a correction would not be necessary. In the remaining paragraphs, we assume that errors discovered are material and should be corrected.

As mentioned previously, preparing the trial balance is one of the primary ways to discover errors in the ledger. However, it indicates only that the debits and credits are equal. If the two totals of the trial balance are not equal, it is probably due to one or more of the errors described below:

Errors Causing Unequal Trial Balance

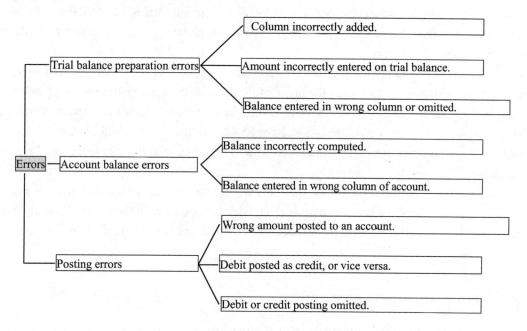

Among the types of errors that will *not* cause the trial balance totals to be unequal are the following:

1. Failure to record a transaction or to post a transaction.
2. Recording the same *erroneous*（错误的）amount for both the debit and the credit parts of a transaction.
3. Recording the same transaction more than once.
4. Posting a part of a transaction correctly as a debit or credit but to the wrong account.

It is obvious that care should be used in recording transactions in the journal and in posting to the accounts. The need for accuracy in determining account balances and reporting them on the trial balance is also *evident*（明显的）.

Errors in the accounts may be discovered in various ways: (1) through audit procedures, (2) by looking at the trial balance or (3) by chance. If the two trial balance totals are not equal, the amount of the difference between the totals should be determined before searching for the error.

The amount of the difference between the two totals of a trial balance sometimes gives a *clue*（线索）as to the nature of the error or where it occurred. For example, a difference of 10,100, or 1,000 between two totals is often the result of an error in addition. A difference between totals can also be due to *omitting*（遗漏）a debit or a credit posting. If the difference can be *evenly*（均

匀地）divided by 2, the error may be due to the posting of a debit as a credit, or *vice versa*（反之亦然）. For example, if the debit total is $20,640 and the credit total is $20,236, the difference of $404 may indicate that a credit posting of $404 was omitted or that a credit of $202 was incorrectly posted as a debit.

Two other common types of errors are known as *transpositions*（数字错位）and *slides*（移位）. A transposition occurs when the order of the digits is changed mistakenly, such as writing $542 as $452. In a slide, the entire number is mistakenly moved one or more spaces to the right or the left, such as writing $542.00 as $54.20 or $5,420.00. If an error of either type has occurred and there are no other errors, the difference between the two trial balance totals can be evenly divided by 9.

If an error is not revealed by the trial balance, the steps in the accounting process must be traced, beginning with the last step and working back to the entries in the journal. Usually, errors causing the trial balance totals to be unequal will be discovered before all of the steps are retraced.

 Answer the following questions:

1. What is one of the primary ways to discover errors in the ledger?
2. Which errors will *not* cause the trial balance totals to be unequal?
3. Describe a transposition.
4. Use an example to define "Slide".
5. List the errors may cause unequal trial balance.

Chapter 3　Journalizing and Posting Transactions
（记账和过账）

导学：前面两章对会计的基本理论和复式记账法做了介绍，其重点是"为何"而不是"如何"进行会计处理，我们的目标是理解编制会计分录的原因以及 T 型账中记录的经济业务的性质。然而，前几章中所借助的会计分录方式既不能提供某一经济业务的必要信息，也不能显示经济业务的序时性记录。为了弥补这些缺陷，会计人员可以使用日记账对整个经济业务过程进行记录。本章将对日记账（journal）、在日记账中编制会计分录（journalizing）以及根据编好的会计分录登记分类账（posting）进行具体介绍。

 Section I　Accounting Study（会计学习）

3.1　The Journal
（日记账）

In the chapters of the text so far, the nature of accounting and the double entry bookkeeping aspects of various transactions have been considered. The primary emphasis was the "why" rather than the "how" of accounting operations; we aimed at an understanding of the reason for making the entry in a particular way as well as of the effects of transactions by making entries in T accounts. However, these entries do not provide the necessary data for a particular transaction, nor do they show a chronological record of transactions. Therefore, in order to make up for these defects and maintain a permanent record of an entire transaction, the accountant can use a book or record known as a ***journal***.

The Journal

The ***journal*** is the initial book for recording all transactions, or the book of original entry for accounting data. The various transactions are evidenced by sales tickets, purchase invoices, check stubs, and so on. On the basis of this evidence, the transactions are entered in chronological order in the journal. The process is called ***journalizing***. Afterward, the data is transferred or posted from the journal to the ***ledger***, the book of subsequent or secondary entry.

This process is called *posting*.

Types of Journals

A number of different journals may be used in a business. For our purposes, they may be grouped into (1) ***general journals*** and (2) ***special journals***.

- General Journal

The basic form of a journal is the general journal (coded as J) in which all types of business transactions can be recorded. The standard form of general journal is shown below.

General Journal   **Page J-1* (7)**

Date (1)	Description (2)	P. R. (3)	Debit (4)	Credit (5)
200X Oct. 7	Cash	11	$10,000	
	Barbara Lendina, Capital	31		$10,000
	Invested cash in the business (6)			

Major Features of the General Journal. The entries in the general journal according to the numbering in the table above are described as follows:

(1) ***Date.*** The year, month, and day of the first entry are written in the date column. The year and month do not have to be repeated for the additional entries until a new month occurs or a new page is needed.

(2) ***Description.*** The account title to be debited is entered on the first line, next to the date column. The name of the account to be credited is entered on the line below and indented.

(3) ***P.R. (Posting Reference).*** Nothing is entered in this column until the particular entry is posted, that is, until the amounts are transferred to the related ledger accounts. The posting process will be described in 3.3.

(4) ***Debit.*** The debit amount for each account is entered in this column. Generally, there is only one item, but there could be two or more separate items.

(5) ***Credit.*** The credit amount for each account is entered in this column. Here again, there is generally only one account, but there could be two or more accounts involved with different amounts.

(6) ***Explanation.*** A brief description of the transaction is usually made on the line below the credit. Generally, a blank line is left between the explanation and the next entry.

(7) ***Page Number.*** Page number is preprinted and will be used to show the relevant journal page. (Page J-1 denotes general journal, page 1.)

Chapter 3 Journalizing and Posting Transactions（记账和过账）

- Special Journal

Generally speaking, each transaction is recorded by first placing an entry in the general journal and then posting the entry to the related accounts in the general ledger. This system, however, is time-consuming and wasteful. It is much simpler and more efficient to group together those transactions that are repetitive, such as sales, purchases, cash receipts, and cash payments, and place each of them in a special journal.

A special journal is designed to record a specific type of frequently occurring business transaction. Most company use, in addition to a general journal, at least the following special journals:

Name of Special Journal	Abbreviation	Type of Transaction
Cash receipts journal	CR	All cash received
Cash disbursements journal	CD	All cash paid out
Purchases journal	P	All purchases on account
Sales journal	S	All sales on account

These four types of special journals are exemplified below:

Cash Receipts Journal CR-1

Date	Account Credited	P. R.	Cash Debit	Sales Discount Debit	Accounts Receivable Credit	Sales Income Credit	Sundry Credit
Dec.1	Purchase Returns		250				250
3	Cash Sales		350			350	
7	Anderson		50		50		
15	Butler		350		350		
21	Cash Sales		200			200	
28	Chase		100		100		
			1,300		500	550	250

Cash Disbursement Journal   CD-1

Date	Check No.	Account Debit	P. R.	Cash Credit	Purchases Discount Credit	Accounts payable Debit	Sundry Debit
Mar. 1	188	Rent Expense		600			600
7	189	Store Supplies		150			150
12	190	Salaries Expense		740			740
16	191	Agin Co.		1,176	24	1,200	
27	192	Walk Co.		500		500	
29	193	Purchases		750			750
30	194	Salaries Expense		810			810
				4,726	24	1,700	3,050

Sales Journal   S-1

Date	Account Debited	P. R.	Amount
Feb. 1	A. Anderson		$200
2	B. Butler		350
12	C. Chase		125
24	D. Davis and Co.		400
			$1,075

Purchases Journal   P-1

Date	Account Credited	P. R.	Accounts Payable Credit	Purchases Debit	Supplies Debit	Sundry Accounts Debited	P. R.	Amount
Feb.1	Agin Co.		1,000	1,000				
2	Walk Co.		500		500			
4	Nant Co.		9,000			Equipment		9,000
12	Davis Co.		11,000			Land		11,000
17	Walk Co.		200		200			
24	Agin Co.		2,000	2,000				
			23,700	3,000	700			20,000

The special journal is used in businesses with a large number of repetitive transactions. A general journal is used for recording transactions that do not fit into the four types illustrated above, that is, all cash received, all cash paid out, all purchases on account and all sales on account. Besides, the general journal is also used for the recording of adjusting and closing entries at the end of the accounting period.

New Words, Phrases and Special Terms

account credited		会计贷项
account debited		会计借项
cash sales		现销
cash disbursements journal		现金支出日记账
cash receipts journal		现金收入日记账
check stub		支票存根
chronological	adj.	按时间顺序的
chronological record		序时记录
evidence	vt.	证明
exemplify	vt.	例证,例示,作为……例子
general journal		普通日记账
general ledger		总分类账
invoice	n.	发票
journal	n.	日记账
journalize	v.	记入日记账
journalizing	n.	登记日记账;(在日记账中)作会计分录
ledger	n.	分类账
permanent	adj.	永久的
P.R. (Posting Reference)		账户编号
purchases discount		购货折扣
purchases journal		购货日记账
purchase returns		购货退回
rent expense		租金,租赁费用
salaries expense		工资费用
sales journal		销售日记账
sales discount		销售折扣
sales income		销售收入
special journal		特种日记账
store supplies		库存商品
sundry	n. a.	其他

T accounts　　　　　　　　　　　　　　T 型账（注：在中国也称为丁字型账）
time-consuming　　　adj.　　　　　　浪费的，糟蹋的
wasteful　　　　　　　adj.　　　　　　费时的，拖延时间的

 Notes

1. The primary emphasis was the "why" rather than the "how" of accounting operations; we aimed at an understanding of the reason for making the entry in a particular way as well as of the effects of transactions by making entries in T accounts.

前面两章的重点是"为何"而不是"如何"进行会计业务处理；我们的目的是既要理解以某种方式编制会计分录的原因，更要理解如何利用 T 型账编制会计分录来反映经济业务的结果。

2. The journal is the initial book for recording all transactions, or the book of original entry for accounting data.

日记账是对所有经济业务的最初记录或是会计资料的原始记录簿。

journal　日记账。由于交易的入账首先在日记账中进行，因此，又把日记账称为原始记录簿（book of original entry）。

3. Generally speaking, each transaction is recorded by first placing an entry in the general journal and then posting the entry to the related accounts in the general ledger.

一般说来，任何一项经济业务都是先在普通日记账作分录，然后再将分录过入总分类账。

4. special journal　特种日记账，旨在记录某一经常发生的特定类型交易。其记录内容有：现金收入（包括现销（all cash received））；现金付出（包括现购（all cash paid out））；赊销（all sales on account）；商品和其他项目（物料、固定资产等）的赊购（all purchases on account）。那些不经常发生、不宜设置特种日记账登记的交易，登记在普通日记账中。

5. Besides, the general journal is also used for the recording of adjusting and closing entries at the end of the accounting period.

除此之外，普通日记账也用于在会计期末进行调账和结账分录的编制。

3.2　Journalizing

（登记日记账）

Journalizing

The recording of transactions in the journal using the double-entry system is called *journalizing*. That is, to record the entire business transaction in chronological order in the journal and embody all the necessary information and effects.

Chapter 3 Journalizing and Posting Transactions (记账和过账)

Procedure of Journalizing

Recording a business transaction in a journal (journalizing) includes two steps:

(1) Analyze transactions from source documents.

Source documents are the business papers that support the existence of business transactions. Source documents take the form of checks, invoices, bills etc. They are used as the basis of recording transactions. All information used in accounting must be evidenced by a source document that identifies the actual cost agreed upon by the buyer and the seller at the time of the transaction.

(2) Record transactions in a journal under the double-entry system.

Business transactions will be recorded in the journal in chronological order. Here, we use the general journal. As is shown in the first table in 3.1, the general journal consists of seven parts, which the recording or journalizing should fulfill: date; the account to be debited and the amount; the account to be credited and the amount; the explanation; the posting reference to the General Ledger and page number. It is to notice that for each transaction, the debit account and its amount are entered first; the credit account and its amount are written below the debit portion.

The following example, which shows how transactions are recorded, can help in understanding the operation of the general journal.

Example 1

Journalize the transactions described for Mr. Drew's law practice.

During the month of January, Ted Drew, Lawyer

Jan. 1 Invested $4,000 to open his practice.
    4 Bought supplies (stationery, forms, pencils, and so on) for cash, $300.
    5 Bought office furniture from Robinson Furniture Company on account, $2,000.
  15 Received $2,500 in fees earned during the month.
  30 Paid office rent for January, $500.
  30 Paid salary for part-time help, $200.
  31 Paid $1,200 to Robinson Furniture Company on account.
  31 After taking an inventory at the end of the month, Drew found that he had used $200 worth of supplies.
  31 Withdrew $400 for personal use.

Date	Description	P.R.	Debit	Credit
200X				
Jan. 1	Cash		4,000	
	T. Drew, Capital			4,000

(continued)

		Investment in law practice		
4		Supplies	300	
		Cash		300
		Bought supplies for cash		
5		Furniture	2,000	
		Accounts Payable		2,000
		Bought furniture from Robinson Furniture Co.		
15		Cash	2,500	
		Fees Income		2,500
		Received payment for services		
30		Rent Expense	500	
		Cash		500
		Paid rent for month		
30		Salaries Expense	200	
		Cash		200
		Paid salaries of part-time help		
31		Accounts Payable	1,200	
		Cash		1,200
		Payment on account to Robinson Furniture Co.		
31		Supplies Expense	200	
		Supplies		200
		Supplies used during month		
31		T. Drew, Drawing	400	
		Cash		400
		Personal withdrawal		

Chapter 3 Journalizing and Posting Transactions（记账和过账）

 New Words, Phrases and Special Terms

bill	n.	账单，钞票，票据，清单
business papers		商业文件
drawing	n.	提款
fees income		规费收入
indent	vt.	定货
source documents		原始凭证
stationery	n.	文具；信纸及信封
supplies expense		物料用品费用

Notes

1. The year and month do not have to be repeated for the additional entries until a new month occurs or a new page is needed.

（日记账中的）年和月在此之后的分录中没必要重复记载，除非出现一个新的月份或需要一张新的账页。

2. Generally, a blank line is left between the explanation and the next entry.

通常注释与下一个分录之间要空出一行。

3. 会计循环中的步骤包括：(1) 根据原始凭证分析交易；(2) 在日记账中记录交易的结果；(3) 过账；(4) 试算平衡；(5) 调整某些账户余额；(6) 编制财务报表；(7) 结清暂时性账户；(8) 转回某些调整分录。在本章我们讨论了会计循环中的前三个步骤。

4. source document 原始凭证。根据公认会计准则中的客观性原则（Objectivity Principle），在日记账中登记交易时，会计人员必须以原始凭证为客观依据，以保证财务信息的真实性。

5. bought supplies for cash 用现金购买物资；payment on account to Robinson Furniture Co. （通过银行）转账支付给罗宾逊家具公司。

3.3 Posting

（过账）

Posting

The process of transferring information from the journal to the ledger for the purpose of summarizing is called ***posting***.

Procedure of Posting

Posting is ordinarily carried out in the following steps:

(1) Record the amount and date. The date and the amounts of the debits and credits are entered in the appropriate accounts.

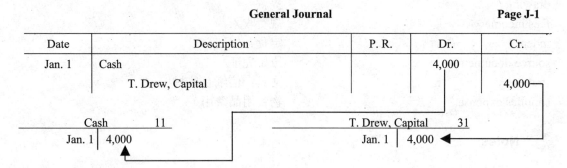

(2) Record the posting reference in the account. The number of the journal page is entered in the account (broken arrows below).

(3) Record the posting in the journal. For cross-referencing, the code number of the account is now entered in the P.R. column of the journal (solid arrows). These numbers are called post reference or folio numbers.

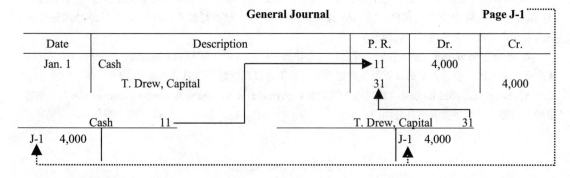

The following example shows how to post accounting data from the journal to the ledger.

Example 2

The results of the posting from the journal appear below.

Chapter 3 Journalizing and Posting Transactions（记账和过账）

```
        Assets              =        Liabilities          +         Capital
          Cash         11        Accounts Payable    21       T. Drew, Capital    31
Jan. 1  4,000 | Jan. 4   300     Jan. 31  1,200 | Jan. 5  2,000            | Jan.1  4,000
     15 2,500 |      30  500                    |         800
 3,900  6,500 |      30  200                                  T. Drew, Drawing    32
              |      31 1,200                               Jan. 31  400 |
              |      31  400
              |         2,600                                 Fees Income         41
                                                                          | Jan. 15  2,500
        Supplies       12
Jan. 4   300 | Jan. 31  200                                   Rent Expense        51
  100                                                       Jan. 30  500 |

        Furniture      13                                   Salaries Expense      52
Jan. 5  2,000 |                                             Jan. 30  200 |

                                                            Supplies Expense      53
                                                            Jan. 31  200 |
```

T. Drew
Trial Balance
January 31, 200X

	Debit	Credit
Cash	$3,900	
Supplies on Hand	100	
Furniture	2,000	
Accounts Payable		$800
T. Drew, Capital		4,000
T. Drew, Drawing	400	
Fees Income		2,500
Rent Expense	500	
Salaries Expense	200	
Supplies Expense	200	
	$7,300	$7,300

New Words, Phrases and Special Terms

folio	n.	（原稿的）一页，页码或张数
post	v.	过账，誊账
posting	n.	过账
supplies on hand		在用物料

Notes

1. The process of transferring information from the journal to the ledger for the purpose of summarizing is called posting. 过账就是将日记账上的每一个分录按照原来的借贷方向，分别转记到分类账的各有关账户中的一种会计处理。
2. record the amount and date 记录金额和日期
3. record the posting reference in the account 在账户中记录编号
4. record the posting in the journal 在日记账中记录过账

Section II Review & Exercises（复习与练习）

 Summary

1. The initial book for recording all transactions is known as the _____.
2. Another name and description of the _____ is book of original entry.
3. The _____ is the book of subsequent or secondary entry.
4. The process of recording transactions in the journal is termed _____.
5. _____ are the business papers that support the existence of business transactions.
6. The process of transferring information from the journal to the ledger is known as_____.

 **Questions**

1. What are the two journal types?
2. What are the types of special journals?
3. How to journalize business transactions?
4. How to post the accounting data to the ledger?

 Solved Problems

1. On the line below each entry, write a brief explanation of the transaction that might appear in the general journal.

		Debit	Credit
(1)	Equipment	10,000	
	Cash		2,000
	Accounts Payable, William Smith		8,000

(continued)

		Debit	Credit
(2)	Accounts Payable, William Smith	8,000	
	Notes Payable		8,000
(3)	Notes Payable	8,000	
	Cash		8,000

2. Dr. R. Berg, Dentist, began his practice, investing in the business the following assets:

        Cash $12,000
        Supplies   1,400
        Equipment   22,600
        Furniture   10,000

Record the opening entry in the journal.

	Debit	Credit

3. If, in Problem 2, Dr. Berg owned a balance of $3,500 on the equipment, what would the opening entry then be?

	Debit	Credit

4. Record the following entries in the general journal for the Stephenson Cleaning Company:

(1) Invested $10,000 cash in the business.

(2) Paid $2,000 for office furniture.
(3) Bought equipment costing $6,000 on account.
(4) Received $2,200 in cleaning income.
(5) Paid one-fourth of the amount owed on the equipment.

	Debit	Credit
(1)		
(2)		
(3)		
(4)		
(5)		

5. Record the following entries in the general journal for the Gavis Medical Group.

(1) Invested $18,000 in cash, $4,800 in supplies, and $12,200 in equipment (of which there is owed $7,000) to begin the Medical Group.
(2) Received $2,400 from cash patients for the week.
(3) Invested additional cash of $5,000 in the firm.
(4) Paid one-half of the amount owed.

	Debit	Credit
(1)		

		(continued)
(2)		
(3)		
(4)		

6. If, in Problem 5, the Gavis Medical Group billed patients for the month for $2,400, and a month later received $1,000, present the necessary journal entries to record each transaction.

	Debit	Credit
(1)		
(2)		

7. On January 1, 200X, Mr. Ling started a dry cleaning service. Record the following entries for the month of January in general journal form. Disregard post reference numbers at this time.

Jan. 1 Invested $5,000 cash and equipment valued at $4,100 to start business.
  12 Paid first month's rent, $400.
  13 Purchased supplies on account, $700.
  16 Received $1,700 for cleaning fees.
  19 Purchased supplies, paying $550 cash.
  21 Paid creditors $500 from Jan. 13 transaction.
  22 Paid electric bill, $275.
  23 Withdrew $500 for personal use.
  25 Received $1,100 for cleaning fees.
  26 Purchased equipment, paying $900 cash.
  28 Sent bills to customers totaling $500 for cleaning fees.

30 Received $300 from Jan. 28 transaction.
30 Paid creditor the balanced owed.

```
     Cash        11          Equipment       17         Notes Payable    22
       |                         |                            |
       |                         |                            |
```

General Journal

Date	Description	P. R.	Debit	Credit
Jan. 1				
12				
13				
16				
19				
21				
22				
23				
25				

				(continued)
Date	Description	P. R.	Debit	Credit
26				
28				
30				
30				

8. Post the following journal entries for the Charles Taxi Company to the T accounts below. Disregard post reference numbers at this time.

		P. R.	Debit	Credit
(1)	Cash		9,000	
	Charles, Capital			9,000
(2)	Equipment		8,000	
	Accounts Payable			4,000
	Cash			4,000
(3)	Accounts Payable		3,000	
	Cash			3,000
(4)	Cash		1,500	
	Fares Income			1,500
(5)	Salaries Expense		600	
	Cash			600

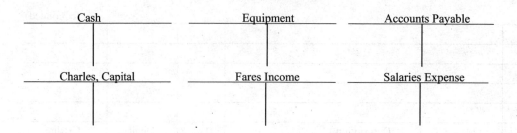

9. Use the balance of the T accounts in Problem 8 to prepare a trial balance.

Charles Taxi Company
Trial Balance

Cash		
Equipment		
Accounts Payable		
Charles, Capital		
Fares Income		
Salaries Expense		

10. From the T accounts below, prepare a trial balance.

```
        Cash                    Capital                  Drawing
  10,000 | 1,000                  | 15,500           1,000 |
   5,000 |                        |  2,000                 |
   6,000 |                                                 
     500 |                                                 


   Rent Expense           Accounts Payable            Notes Payable
     500 |                    500 |   500                  | 1,000
                                  |   600                  |   500
                                  | 1,000


    Equipment                   Land                Accounts Receivable
   2,500 |                   5,000 |                    500 | 1,000
                                                     2,500 |
                                                       200 |
```

Supplies	Fees Income	Wages Expense
300	7,000	1,450
150	9,000	

Ace Hardware Store
Trial Balance
December 31, 200X

Cash		
Accounts Receivable		
Supplies		
Land		
Equipment		
Accounts Payable		
Notes Payable		
Capital		
Drawing		
Fees Income		
Rent Expense		
Wages Expense		

11. The trial balance for Dampman Playhouse on October 31, 200X, was as follows:

Dampman Playhouse
Trial Balance
October 31, 200X

Cash	$2,400	
Accounts Receivable	1,500	
Supplies	350	
Equipment	11,200	
Building	10,000	
Accounts Payable		$9,450
Notes Payable		12,000
Dampman Playhouse, Capital		4,000
	$25,450	$25,450

Selected transactions for November were as follows:

(1) Nov. 2   Paid $1,000 due on the notes payable.
(2)   8   Paid $3,000 on account.
(3)   15   Receipts for the 2-week period totaled $8,400.
(4)   22   Bought an additional projector at a cost of $15,500 with a cash down payment of $5,000, the balance to be paid within 1 year.
(5)   30   Paid salaries of $1,600.

Using this data, (1) transfer the October 31 balances to the ledger accounts, (2) prepare journal entries for the month of November, (3) post to the ledger accounts, and (4) prepare a trial balance.

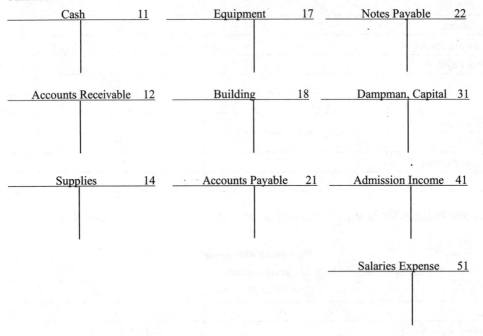

Journal   Page J-6

Date	Description	P. R.	Debit	Credit

(continued)

Dampman Playhouse
Trial Balance
November 30, 200X

Cash		
Accounts Receivable		
Supplies		
Equipment		
Building		
Accounts Payable		
Notes Payable		
Dampman, Capital		
Admissions Income		
Salaries Expense		

Section III Reading Material（阅读材料）

Steps in the Accounting Cycle

The *accounting cycle*（会计循环）(see the following figure: Accounting Cycle) can be divided into the following steps:

(1) Transactions, from information on source documents, are recorded in a journal.
(2) Journal entries are posted to a ledger.
(3) Worksheet, including a trial balance, is prepared from the ledger.
(4) Financial statements are prepared from the worksheet.
(5) Ledger is closed and accounts are balanced and ruled.
(6) Post-closing trial balance of the ledger is taken.

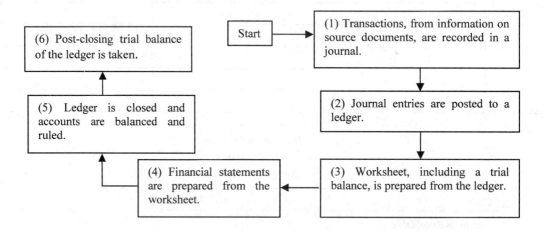

Accounting Cycle

The various steps in the accounting cycle do not occur with equal *frequency*（频繁程度）. Usually, analyzing, journalizing and posting（steps (1)~(3)) take place during each operating period, whereas accounts are adjusted and statements are prepared only when management requires financial statements—usually at monthly or quarterly *intervals*（间隔）, but at least annually. Temporary accounts are *customarily*（通常）closed only at the end of the accounting year.

Business firms whose accounting year ends on December 31 are said to be on a *calendar-year*（日历年度）basis. Many firms prefer to have their accounting year *coincide with*（与……一致）their "natural" business year; thus the year ends when business is slow and inventory quantities are small and easier to count. At this time, end-of-year accounting procedures are most efficiently accomplished. An accounting year ending with a month *other than*（而不是）December is called a *fiscal year*（财务年度）.

Steps in a Merchandise Transaction

Whenever a transaction is *initiated*（开始）for the purchase or sale of merchandise, the buyer and the seller should agree on the price of the merchandise, *the terms of payment*（付款条款）, and which party is to bear the cost of transportation. Most large businesses *fill out*（填写）a *purchase order*（购买订单）when ordering merchandise.

A typical sequence of events is as follows:

(1) A request for a purchase, called a purchase *requisition*（请购单）, is initiated by the person *in charge of*（掌管）merchandise *stock*（存货）records whenever certain items are needed or when quantities of certain merchandise fall below established *reorder points*（再订货点）. The requisition is *forwarded*（递送）to the purchasing department.

(2) The purchasing department then prepares a *purchase order*（订货单）after consulting *price lists* （价目表）*quotations*（行情表）, or suppliers' *catalogs*（供应商商品目录）. The purchase order, addressed to the selected *vendor*（卖主）, indicates the quantity, description, and price of the merchandise ordered. It may also indicate expected terms of payment and arrangements for transportation, including payment of freight costs.

(3) After receiving the purchase order, the seller, upon shipment, *makes out*（开具）an invoice, which is forwarded to the purchaser. The invoice, called a sales *invoice*（销货发票）by the seller and a purchase *invoice*（购货发票）by the buyer, defines the terms of the transaction.

(4) Upon receiving the shipment of merchandise, the purchaser's *receiving department*（收货部门）counts and inspects the items in the shipment and makes out a *receiving report*（收货报告）detailing the quantities received.

(5) Before approving the invoice for payment, either the purchasing department or the accounts payable department compares copies of the purchase order, invoice, and receiving report to determine that quantities, descriptions, and prices are in agreement.

Although all the above papers—purchase requisition, purchase order, receiving report, and invoice—are source documents, only the invoice provides the basis for an entry in the purchaser's accounting records. The other three documents are merely supporting documents. The purchaser makes no entries until the invoice is approved for payment. The seller enters the transaction in the records when the invoice is prepared, usually upon shipment of the merchandise.

Answer the following questions:

1. What are the steps in the accounting cycle?
2. What is a fiscal year?
3. What's the sequence of merchandise transaction?
4. State the purpose of and the key information appearing on each of the following forms:
(1) purchase requisition; (2) purchase order; (3) sales invoice; (4) receiving report.

Chapter 4 Financial Statements
（财务报表）

导学：企业的所有者及经营者需要定期了解两个至关重要的问题：一是企业的净收益（利润）是多少；二是企业的资本有多少。对于这两个问题，会计恒等式所提供的资产、负债及所有者权益之间简单的平衡关系不足以给出完整的解释。我们必须知道会计期间每一笔收入、支出的类别与金额，在期末，还必须明确每种资产、负债及所有者权益的类别与金额。损益表与资产负债表即提供了上述所需的信息。

Section I Accounting Study（会计学习）

4.1 Income Statement
（损益表）

The income statement may be defined as a summary of the revenue (income), expenses, and net income of a business entity for a specific period of time. This may also be called a profit and loss statement, an operating statement, or a statement of operations. Let us review the meanings of the elements entering into the income statement.

Revenue. The increase in capital resulting from the delivery of goods or rendering of services by the business. In amount, the revenue is equal to the cash and receivables gained in compensation for the goods delivered or services rendered.

Expenses. The decrease in capital caused by the business's revenue-producing operations. In amount, the expense is equal to the value of goods and services used up or consumed in obtaining revenue.

Net income. The increase in capital resulting from profitable operation of a business; it is the excess of revenue over expenses for the accounting period.

It is important to note that a cash receipt qualified as revenue only if it serves to increase capital. Similarity, a ***cash payment*** is an expense only if it decreases capital. Thus, for instance, borrowing cash from a bank does not contribute to revenue.

Example 1

Mr. T. Drew's total January income and the totals for his various expenses can be obtained by analyzing the transaction. The income from fees amounted to $2,500, and the expenses incurred to produce this income were: rent, $500; salaries, $200; and supplies, $200. The formal income statement can now be prepared.

T. Drew

Income Statement

Month of January, 200X

Fees Income		$2,500
Operating Expense		
Rent Expense	$500	
Salaries Expenses	200	
Supplies Expenses	<u>200</u>	
Total Operating Expenses		<u>900</u>
Net Income		<u>$1,600</u>

In many companies, there are hundreds and perhaps thousands of income and expenses transactions in a month. To lump all these transactions under one account would be very cumbersome and would, in addition, make it impossible to show relationships among the various items. For example, we might wish to know the relationship of selling expenses to sales and whether the ratio is higher or lower than in previous periods. To solve this problem, we set up a temporary set of income and expense accounts. The net difference of these accounts, the net profit or net loss, is then transferred as one figure to the capital account.

Accrual Basis and Cash Basis of Accounting

Because an income statement pertains to a definite period of time, it becomes necessary to determine just when an item of revenue or expense is to be accounted for. Under the ***accrual basis*** of accounting, revenue is recognized only when it is earned and expense is recognized only when it is incurred. This differs significantly from the ***cash basis*** of accounting, which recognizes revenue and expense generally with the receipt and payment of cash. Essential to the accrual basis is the matching of expenses with the revenue that they help produce. Under the accrual system, the accounts are adjusted at the end of the accounting period to properly reflect the revenue earned and the cost and expenses applicable to the period.

Most business firms use the accrual basis, whereas individuals and professional people generally use the cash basis. Ordinarily, the cash basis is not suitable when there are significant amounts of inventories, receivables, and payables.

 New Words, Phrases and Special Terms

adjust	vt.	调整，调节
applicable	adj.	可适用的，可应用的
cash basis		收付实现制（以现金为依据的记账法）
cash payment		现金支付
cash receipt		现金收入
compensation	n.	补偿，赔偿
determine	v.	决定，确定
essential	n.	本质，实质
incur	v.	招致
lump	vt.	集中，汇总，混在一起
obtain	vt.	获得，得到
payables	n.	应付款项
pertain to		属于，关于
qualify	v.	（使）具有资格，符合要求
receivables	n.	应收款项，应收票据
salary	n.	薪水，薪金
significant	adj.	有意义的，重要的
supply	n. v.	供给，补给，存货
temporary	adj.	暂时的，临时的
transfer	v.	转移，转账

 Notes

1. The income statement may be defined as a summary of the revenue (income), expenses, and net income of a business entity for a specific period of time. This may also be called a profit and loss statement, an operating statement, or a statement of operations.

收益表可以定义为经营单位在特定时期内的收入（收益）、费用和净收益的汇总，又称为损益表或营业报表。

2. It is important to note that a cash receipt qualified as revenue only if it serves to increase capital.

需要注意的是只有当现金收入导致资本增加的情况下才记为收益项。

3. To lump all these transaction under one account would be very cumbersome and would, in addition, make

it impossible to show relationships among the various items.

把所有这些交易集中在一个账户中非常烦琐，同时也无法反映出各个项目之间的关系。

4. Under the accrual system, the accounts are adjusted at the end of the accounting period to properly reflect the revenue earned and the cost and expenses applicable to the period.

根据权责发生制，在会计期末要调整账目使之能准确地反映当期收入和成本、费用的情况。

5. accrual basis of accounting 权责发生制。它与收付实现制（cash basis of accounting）一起，是现代会计中确定收入和费用的两大基础。根据收付实现制，企业的收入实现与费用发生的确认时间，应在与收入和费用相关的现金收到或支付之时。权责发生制是流行的会计惯例，详细内容请见 Chapter 5。

6. Financial Statement 财务报表。企业应编制的财务报表包括资产负债表、损益表、现金流量表（Statement of Cash Flows）三种基本报表，其他报表为基本报表的副表。本章着重介绍资产负债表、损益表及其副表。

4.2 Balance Sheet
（资产负债表）

The information needed for the balance sheet items are the net balances at the end of the period, rather than the total for the period as in the income statement. Thus, management wants to know the balance of cash in the bank, the balance of inventory, equipment, and so on, on hand at the end of the period.

The balance sheet may thus be defined as a statement showing the assets, liabilities, and capital of a business entity at a specific date. This statement is also called a statement of financial position or a statement of financial condition.

In preparing a balance sheet, it is not necessary to make any further analysis of the data. The needed data—that is, the balances of the asset, liability, and capital accounts—are already available.

Example 2　Report Form

T. Drew
Balance Sheet
January 31, 200X

ASSETS

Cash	$3,900
Supplies	100
Furniture	2,000
Total Assets	$6,000

LIABILITIES AND CAPITAL

Liabilities			
Accounts Payable			$800
Capital			
Balance, January 1, 200X		$4,000	
Net Income for January	$1,600		
Less: Withdrawals	400		
Increase in Capital		1,200	
Total Capital			5,200
Total Liabilities and Capital			$6,000

The close relationship of the income statement and the balance sheet is apparent. The net income of $1,600 for January, shown as the final figure on the income statement of Example 1, is also shown as a separate figure on the balance sheet of Example 2. The income statement is thus the connecting link between two balance sheets. As discussed earlier, the income and expense items are actual a further analysis of the capital account.

The balance sheet of Example 2 is arranged in report form, with the liabilities and capital sections shown below the asset section. It may also be arranged in account form, with the liabilities and capital sections to the right of, rather than below, the asset section, as shown in Example 3.

Example 3   Account Form

T. Drew
Balance Sheet
January 31, 200X

ASSETS			LIABILITIES AND CAPITAL			
Cash	$3,900		Liabilities			
Supplies	100		Accounts Payable			$800
Furniture	2,000		Capital			
			Balance, January 1, 200X		$4,000	
			Net Income for January	$1,600		
			Less: Withdrawals	400		
			Increase in Capital		1,200	
			Total Capital			5,200
Total Assets	$6,000		Total Liabilities and Capital			$6,000

4.3 Capital Statement
(资本变动表)

Instead of showing the details of the capital account in the balance sheet, we may show the changes in separate form called the capital statement, or the statement of owner's equity.

Example 4

T. Drew
Balance Sheet
January 31, 200X

Capital, January 1, 200X		$4,000
Net Income for January	$1,600	
Less: Withdrawals	400	
Increase in Capital		1,200
Total Capital		$5,200

In the sole proprietorships and partnerships, the capital statement, or a statement of owners' equity is frequently prepared to accompany the balance sheet and income statement. This is simply a summary of the changes in the owners' capital balance during the accounting period. The following exhibit shows this type of statement for Douglas Trading Company. Note that the ending balance on this statement agrees with the owners' capital balance on the balance sheet on Jan.31, 200X.

Example 5

DOUGLAS TRADING COMPANY
Statement of Owner's Equity
for the Month Ended Jan.31, 200X

K. Douglas, Capital, Jan.1		$120,000
Add: Capital Contributed in January	$40,000	
Net Income for January	36,000	76,000
		$196,000
Less: Capital Withdrawn in January		16,000
K. Douglas, Capital, Jan.31		$180,000

This statement further demonstrates the relationship between the income statement and the balance sheet. The net income (or net loss) for a period in income statement is an input into the statement of owners' equity, while the ending owners' equity balance on this statement is an input into the balance sheet at the end of the period.

New Words, Phrases and Special Terms

analysis	n.	分析，分解
apparent	adj.	明显的，显而易见的
available	adj.	可用到的，可利用的
capital statement		资本变动表
entity	n.	实体，组织
furniture	n.	家具，设备
section	n.	部分，区
sole proprietorships		独资企业

 Notes

1. The balance sheet may thus be defined as a statement showing the assets, liabilities, and capital of a business entity at a specific date. This statement is also called a statement of financial position or a statement of financial condition.

资产负债表是反映某一特定日期经营单位的资产、负债和所有者权益的报表。资产负债表又称财务状况表。

2. Instead of showing the details of the capital account in the balance sheet, we may show the changes in separate form called the capital statement.

除了在资产负债表中反映资本账户的详细情况以外，还可以另设一张单独报表来反映资本账户的变化情况，该报表称为资本变动表。

3. The net income (or net loss) for a period in income statement is an input into the statement of owners' equity, while the ending owners' equity balance on this statement is an input into the balance sheet at the end of the period.

收益表中某会计期间的净收益（或净亏损）是业主权益表中的一个输入项（加项或减项），而业主权益表中的期末业主权益余额则是进入期末资产负债表的一个项目。

4.4　Financial Statement Summary
（财务报表概述）

The three financial statements from Example 2, 3, and 4 are interrelated as shown in Example 6.

Example 6

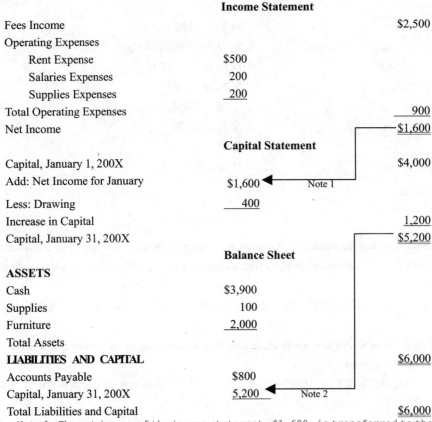

Note 1. The net income of the income statement, $1,600, is transferred to the capital statement.
Note 2. The capital is summarized in the capital statement and the final balance included in the balance sheet.

4.5 Classified Financial Statements
（分类财务报表）

Financial statements become more useful when the individual items are classified into significant groups for comparison and financial analysis.

The Income Statement

The classified income statement sets out the amount of each function and enables management, stockholders, analysts, and others to study the changes in function costs over successive accounting periods. There are three functional classifications of the income statement.

(1) **Revenue**. Revenue includes gross income from the sale of products or services. It may be designated as sales, income from fees, and so on, to indicate gross income. The gross amount is reduced by sales returns and by sales discounts to arrive at net sales.

(2) *Cost of goods sold*. The inventory of a merchandising business consists of goods on hand at the beginning of the accounting period and those on hand at the end of the accounting period. The beginning inventory appears in the income statement (Cost of Goods Sold Section, also known as GOGS) and is added to purchases to arrive at the cost of goods available for sale. The ending inventory is deducted from the cost of goods available for sale to arrive at cost of goods sold.

(3) *Operating expenses*. Operating expenses includes all expenses or resources consumed in obtaining revenue. Operating expenses are further divided into two groups. Selling expenses are those related to the promotion and sale of the company's product or service. Generally, one individual is held accountable for this function, and his or her performance is measured by the results in increasing sales and maintaining selling expenses at an established level. General and administrative expenses are those related to the overall activities of the business, such as the salaries of the president and other officers. When preparing income statements, list expenses from highest to lowest except Miscellaneous, which is always last, no matter how large the amount may be.

Example 7

J. C. Company
Income Statement
Year Ended June 30, 200X

Sales			$39,800
Cost of Goods Sold:			
Inventory (Beginning)		$ 2,700	
Purchases		17,200	
Goods Available for Sale		$19,900	
Less: Inventory (Ending)		2,900	
Cost of Goods Sold		$ 2,700	
			17,000
			$22,800
Operating Expenses:			
Salaries Expenses		$11,400	
Advertising Expenses		2,300	
General Expenses		2,000	

Total Operating Expenses	15,700
Net Profit	$ 7,100

The Balance Sheet

The balance sheet becomes a more useful statement for comparison and financial analysis if the asset and liability groups are classified. For example, an important index of the financial state of a business, which can be derived from the classified balance sheet, is the ratio of current assets to current liabilities. This current ratio ought, generally, to be at least 2:1; that is, current assets should be twice current liabilities. For our purposes, we will designate the following classifications:

Assets

Current asset
Property, plant, and equipment
Other assets

Liabilities

Current liabilities
Long-term liabilities

Current assets. Assets are reasonably expected to be converted into cash or used in the current operation of the business. (The current period is generally taken as 1 year.) Examples are cash, notes receivable, accounts receivable, inventory, and prepaid expenses (prepaid insurance, prepaid rent, and so on). List these current assets in order of liquidity.

Property, plant, and equipment. Long-lived assets used in the production of goods or services. These assets, sometimes called *fixed assets* or *plant assets,* are used in the operation of the business rather than being held for sale, as are inventory items.

Other assets. Various assets other than current assets, fixed assets, or assets to which specific captions are given. For instance, the caption "investments" would be used if significant sums were invested. Often, companies show a caption for intangible assets such as patents or goodwill. In other cases, there may be a separate caption for deferred charges. If, however, the amounts are not large in relation to total assets, the various items may be grouped under one caption, "Other Assets".

Current liabilities. Debts that must be satisfied from current assets within the next operating period, usually 1 year. Examples are accounts payable, notes payable, the current portion of long-term debt, and various accrued items such as salaries payable and taxes payable.

Long-term liabilities. Liabilities that are payable beyond the next year. The most common examples are bonds payable and mortgages payable. Example 8 shows a classified balance sheet of typical form.

Example 8

F. Satlzmann
Balance Sheet
January 31, 200X

ASSETS			
Current Assets			
Cash		$5,400	
Accounts Receivable		1,600	
Supplies		500	
Total Current Assets			$7,500
Fixes Assets			
Land		$4,000	
Building		8,000	
Equipment		2,000	
Total Fixed Assets			14,000
Total Assets			$21,500
LIABILITIES AND CAPITAL			
Current Liabilities			
Accounts Payable		$2,000	
Notes Payable		1,750	
Total Current Liabilities			$ 3,750
Long-Term Liabilities			
Mortgage Payable			1,2000
Total Liabilities			$15,750
Capital			
F. Saltzmann, Capital, January 1		$4,750	
Net Income for the Year	$3,000 *		
Less: Withdrawals	2,000		
Increase in Capital		1,000	
F. Satlzmann, Capital, December 31			5,750
Total Liabilities and Capital			$21,500

* Assumed.

 New Words, Phrases and Special Terms

accountable   adj.   应负责的，有责任的

administrative expenses		管理费用
analyst	n.	分析人士，分解者
caption	n.	标题，说明
classify	vt.	分类，分等
comparison	n.	比较，对照
consists of		由……组成，含有
consume	v.	消耗，消费
convert into		折合，转化为
cost of goods sold		销货成本
current asset		流动资产
current liability		流动负债
defer	v.	推迟，延期
derive from		获得，导出
designate	v.	指明，指派
established	adj.	既定的，确定的
gross income		总收入，总收益，毛收入
index	n.	指数，指标，索引
indicate	vt.	指出，显示
individual	adj.	个别的，单独的
interrelated	adj.	相互关联的
liquidity	n.	变现能力，流动性
merchandising	n.	商品销售
miscellaneous	n.	杂项，其他
mortgage	n.	抵押，按揭
notes receivable		应收票据
operating expenses		营业费用，营运费用
prepaid expense		预付费用
promotion	n.	促销，提升
property	n.	财产，所有物，所有权
ratio	n.	比例，比率
sales discounts		销货折扣
sales returns		销货退回
selling expense		销售费用
stockholder	n.	股东，持股者

Notes

1. The classified income statement sets out the amount of each function and enables management, stockholders, analysts, and others to study the changes in function costs over successive accountin g periods.

分类损益表显示每一项目的金额，使管理者、股东、分析人士和其他人士在连续的会计期间研究各种运营成本的变化。

2. The inventory of a merchandising business consists of goods on hand at the beginning of the accounting period and those on hand at the end of the accounting period.

一个商品销售企业的库存商品包括会计期初的库存商品和会计期末的库存商品。

3. Generally, one individual is held accountable for this function, and his or her performance is measured by the results in increasing sales and maintaining selling expenses at an established level.

通常应有专人对此负责，其业绩通过他（她）所提高的销售额及将销售费用控制在既定水平的成效来衡量。

4. For example, an important index of the financial state of a business, which can be derived from the classified balance sheet, is the ratio of current assets to current liabilities.

比如，企业财务状况的一个重要指数——流动资产与流动负债之比（流动比率）就可从分类资产负债表中获得。

5. When preparing income statements, list expenses from highest to lowest except Miscellaneous, which is always last, no matter how large the amount may be.

在创建损益表时，支出项目应根据金额从高至低列出，而杂项除外，不管其金额多大都列在最后。

 Section II Review & Exercises（复习与练习）

 Summary

1. Another term for an accounting report is an _____.
2. The statement that shows net income for the period is known as the _____ statement.
3. The statement that shows net loss for the period is known as the _____ statement.
4. Two groups of items that make up the income statement are _____ and _____.
5. The difference between income and expense is known as _____.
6. Withdrawal of money by the owner is not an expense but a reduction of _____.

7. To show the change in capital of a business, the _____ statement is used.
8. The balance sheet contains _____, _____, and _____.
9. Assets must equal _____.
10. Expense and income must be matched in the same _____.

Questions

1. What is the purpose of preparing for a balance sheet?
2. What is the purpose of preparing for an income statement?
3. Explain the complementary relationship between the balance sheet and income statement.
4. What is meant by "accrual basis and cash basis of accounting"?
5. What are the significant groups in classified financial statements?

Solved problems

1. Below is an income statement with some of the information missing. Fill in the information needed to complete the income statement.

Sales Income		(2)
Operating Expense		
Wages Expense	$16,910	
Rent Expenses	(1)	
Utilities Expenses	3,150	
Total Operating Expenses		32,150
Net Income		$41,300

2. The following information was taken from an income statement:

Fees Income	$14,000
Rent Expense	2,000
Salary Expense	5,000
Miscellaneous Expenses	1,000

If the owner withdrew $2,000 from the firm, what is the increase or decrease in capital?

(continued)

3. Based on the information in Problem 2, if the withdrawal were $9,000 instead of $2,000, what would the increase (decrease) become?

4. Place a check mark in the appropriate box below to indicate the name of the account group in which each account belongs.

	Income Statement		Balance Sheet		
	Income	Expense	Assets	Liability	Capital
Accounts Payable					
Accounts Receivable					
Building					
Capital					
Cash					
Drawing					
Equipment					
Fees Income					
General Expense					
Interest Expense					
Interest Income					
Land					
Notes Payable					
Other Income					
Rent Expense					
Rent Income					
Salaries Expense					
Supplies					
Supplies Expense					
Tax Expense					

5. Prepare a balance sheet as of December 31, 200X, from the following data:

Accounts Payable	$3,000
Cash	4,000
Equipment	16,000
Notes Payable	12,000
Supplies	200
Net Income	11,400
Drawing	10,200
Capital, January 1, 200X	4,000

ASSETS		
Cash		
Supplies		
Equipment		
Total Assets		
LIABILITIES AND CAPITAL		
Accounts Payable		
Notes Payable		
Total Liabilities		
Capital, December 31, 200X*		
*CAPITAL STATEMENT		

6. Classify the following accounts by placing a check mark in the appropriate column.

	Current Asset	Fixed Asset	Current Liability	Long-Term Liability
Accounts Receivable				
Accounts Payable				
Note Payable				
Mortgage Payable				
Cash				

Supplies				
Salaries Payable				
Bonds Payable				
Equipment				
Land				

7. Below are account balances as of December 31, 200X, of R. Dames, owner of a movie theater.

Accounts Payable	$11,400	Film Rental Expense	$6,000
Admission Income	34,200	Miscellaneous Expense	4,000
Capital, January 1, 200X	16,000	Notes Payable	1,000
Cash	7,500	Rent Expense	10,000
Drawing	5,400	Salaries Expense	7,000
Equipment	18,500	Supplies	4,200

Prepare (1) an income statement, (2) a capital statement, (3) a balance sheet.

(1)

R. Dames
Income Statement
Year Ended December 31, 200X

(2)

R. Dames
Capital Statement
Year Ended December 31, 200X

(3)

R. Dames
Balance Sheet
Year Ended December 31, 200X

Section III Reading Material（阅读材料）

Notes to the Financial Statements

The notes to the financial statements are an *integral part*（不可或缺的部分）of the statements. The notes *disclose*（显示）the significant accounting policies used to prepare the financial statements. They also provide additional detail concerning several of the items on the accounting statements.

Subjects typically covered as notes to financial statements in annual reports:

1. More detailed *breakdowns*（细目分类）of other income, interest and other financial charges, and *provision*（条款）for income taxes.

2. A description of the *earnings-per-share*（每股收益）calculation.

3. Details concerning *extraordinary items*（非常项目）, if any, and foreign exchange gains or losses.

4. Breakdown of inventories, investments（including nonconsolidated subsidiaries, property, plant, equipment, and other assets）.

5. Costs and amounts of short-term borrowings.

6. Schedules of long-term debt, *preferred stock*（优先股）, and capitalized and operation

lease obligations.

7. Schedule of *capital stock*(股本)issued or reserved for issuance and statement of changes in shareholders' equity (which is often included as a separate financial statement).

8. Details concerning significant acquisitions or disposals of assets.

9. Information concerning employee *pension* (养老金) and *stock option* (职工优先认股权) plans.

10. *Commitments* (承诺，约定) and *contingent liabilities* (临时负债).

11. Events subsequent to the balance sheet date, but prior to the release of the financial statements to the public, which might significantly affect their *interpretation* (解释).

12. Quarterly operating results.

13. Business segment information (by line of business and by geographic region).

14. A five-year summary comparison of financial performance and financial position.

Published annual reports also include management's discussion of recent operating results. Management's discussion is included along with the financial statements. Usually there is also a letter to the stockholders, which appears at the front of the annual report. This letter and the management's discussion can help you interpret the accounting statements. They can also provide *insights* (洞察) into management's philosophy and strategy.

 Answer the following questions:

1. What is the note to the financial statements?
2. What is the importance of adding the note to the financial statements?
3. List the major subjects typically covered as notes to financial statements.
4. Give more examples of extraordinary items.
5. State the major parts published annual reports also include.

Chapter 5 Adjusting and Closing Procedures
（调账和结账）

导学： 会计是一个通过对企业的经济业务进行处理，从而为会计信息使用者提供财务报告的信息系统。完善的会计信息系统下的会计处理是按照一定的步骤在一个个会计期间内周而复始、循环往复的。在会计循环中，日常经济业务通过会计分录记入分类账，由于财务会计的确认标准是权责发生制，分类账中会有一些跨越几个会计期间的交易及事项，则在所属期间确认时就有可能发生错误，因此我们需要对这些经济业务的记录进行调整处理，这一过程称为调账（adjusting）。此外，在会计期末为了真实反映企业的财务状况，需要将一切与损益表相关的账户余额结转到所有者权益类账户中，这一过程称为结账（closing）。

 Section I Accounting Study（会计学习）

5.1 Adjust Entries Covering Recorded Data
（对已入账（会计）记录的调整分录）

Accounting records are kept on an accrual basis, except in the case of very small businesses. ***To accrue*** means to ***collect or accumulate***. This means that revenue is recognized when it is earned, regardless of when cash is actually collected, and expense is matched to the revenue, regardless of when cash is paid out. Most revenue is earned when goods or services are delivered. At this time, title to the goods or services is transferred, and there is created a legal obligation to pay for such goods or services. Some revenue, such as rental income, is recognized on a time basis and is earned when the specified period of time has passed. The accrual concept demands that expenses be kept in step with revenue, so that each month sees only that month's expenses applied against the revenue for that month. The necessary matching is brought about through a type of journal entry. In this chapter, we shall discuss these adjusting entries and also the closing entries through which the adjusted balances are ultimately transferred to balance sheet accounts at the end of the fiscal year.

Adjusting Entries Covering Recorded Data

To adjust expense or income items that have already been recorded, only a reclassification is required; that is, amounts have only to be transferred from one account (for example, Prepaid Insurance) to another (Insurance Expense). The following examples will show how adjusting entries are made for the principal types of recorded expenses.

Examples

1. Prepaid Insurance

Assume that a business paid a $1,200 premium on April 1 for one year's insurance in advance. This represents an increase in one asset (Prepaid Expense) and a decrease in another asset (Cash). Thus, the entry would be:

    Prepaid Insurance 1,200
      Cash   1,200

At the end of April, one-twelfth of the $1,200, or $100, had expired (been used up). Therefore, an adjustment has to be made, decreasing or crediting Prepaid Insurance and increasing or debiting Insurance Expense. The entry would be:

    Insurance Expense 100
      Prepaid Insurance 100

Thus, $100 would be shown as Insurance Expense in the income statement for April, and the balance of $1,100 would be shown as Prepaid Insurance in the balance sheet.

2. Prepaid Rent

Assume that on March 1 a business paid $1,500 to cover rent for the balance of the year. The full amount would have been recorded as a debit to prepaid expense in March. Since there is a 10-month period involved, the rent expense each month is $150. The balance of Prepaid Rent would be $1,350 at the beginning of April. The adjusting entry for April would be:

    Rent Expense   150
      Prepaid Rent   150

At the end of April, the balance in the prepaid rent account would be $1,200.

3. Supplies on Hand

A type of prepayment that is somewhat different from those previously described is the payment for office or factory supplies. Assume that $400 worth of supplies were purchased on April 1. At the end of April, when expense and revenue are to be matched and statements prepared, a count of the amount on hand will be made. Assume that the inventory count shows that $250 of supplies are still on hand. Then the amount consumed during April was $150 ($400

– $250). The two entries would be as follows:

	Apr.	1	Supplies	400	
			Cash		400
		30	Supplies Expense	150	
			Supplies		150

Supplies Expense of $150 will be included in the April income statement; Supplies on Hand of $250 will be included as an asset on the balance sheet of April 30.

In each of the above examples, the net effect of the adjusting entry is to credit the same account as was originally debited. The following examples illustrate what are called *valuation or offset accounts*.

4. Accumulated Depreciation

In the previous three adjusting entries, the balances of the assets mentioned (Prepaid Insurance, Prepaid Rent, and Supplies) were all reduced. These assets usually lose their value in a relatively short period of time. However, assets that have a longer life expectancy (such as a building, equipment, etc.) are treated differently because the accounting profession wants to keep a balance sheet record of the equipment's original (historical) cost. Thus the adjusting entry needed to reflect the true value of the long-term asset each year must allocate (spread) the cost of its original price. This spreading concept is known as *depreciation*. In order to accomplish the objectives of keeping the original cost of the equipment and also maintaining a running total of the depreciation allocated, we must create a new account *entitled* Accumulated Depreciation. This account is known as a *contra asset* (which has the opposite balance of its asset), and it summarizes and accumulates the amount of depreciation over the equipment's total useful life. Assume that machinery costing $15,000 was purchased on February 1 of the current year and was expected to last 10 years. With the straight-line method of accounting (i.e., equal charges each period), the depreciation would be $1,500 a year, or $125 a month. The adjusting entry would be:

Depreciation Expense	125	
Accumulated Depreciation		125

At the end of April, Accumulated Depreciation would have a balance of $375, representing 3 months' accumulated depreciation. The account would be shown in the balance sheet as follows:

Machinery		$15,000	
Less: Accumulated Depreciation		375	$14,625

5. Allowance for Uncollectible Accounts

A business with many accounts receivable will reasonably expect to have some losses from uncollectible accounts. It will not be known which specific accounts will not be collected, but past experience furnishes an estimate of the total uncollectible amount.

Assume that a company estimates that 1 percent of sales on account will be uncollectible. Then, if such sales are $10,000 for April, it is estimated that $100 will be uncollectible. The actual loss may not definitely be determined for a year or more, but the loss attributed to April sales would call for an adjusting entry:

    Uncollectible Accounts Expense   100
      Allowance for Uncollectible Accounts   100

If the balance in Accounts Receivable at April 30 was $9,500 and the previous month's balance in Allowance for Uncollectible Accounts was $300, the balance sheet at April 30 would show the following:

  Accounts Receivable $9,500
  Less: Allowance for Uncollectible Accounts   400 $9,100

 New Words, Phrases and Special Terms

accumulated depreciation		累计折旧
accrue	v.	应计，发生权责
adjusting	n.	调整（调账）
adjusted balances		调整后的余额
an accrual basis		权责发生制
allocate	vt.	分配，配给
be used up		被用完，被花光
be matched to		与……相配比
be brought about		由……带来，招致，引起
closing	n.	终结（结账）
call for		要求，需要
deliver	vt.	交付，移交
life expectancy		预计（使用）寿命
expire	vi.	期满，到期
fiscal year		财政年度，财务年度
furnish	vt.	提供，供给
illustrate	vt.	举例说明
in step with		与……同步
insurance	n.	保险

in advance		预先,提前
on a time basis		根据期间原则
obligation	n.	义务,责任
original (historical) cost		原始(历史)成本
offset accounts		净值
prepaid insurance		预付保险费
prepaid rent		预付租金
premium	n.	保险费,额外费用
prepayment	n.	预付费,预付款
previously	adv.	以前,先前
revenue	n.	收入
rental income		租金收入
rent expense		租金费用
reclassification	n.	重分类
supply	n.	原材料,供给
supplies on hand		库存原材料
somewhat	adv.	稍微,有点
title	n.	权利,财产所有权,产权
transfer	vt.	转移,移交
ultimately	adv.	最后,终于,根本地
uncollectible accounts		未收回的账户余额(坏账)
valuation	n.	评估价

Notes

1. adjusting 调账。调账的目的是记录日常经济业务过程中不能正确计量的收入与费用。调账一般是通过调整分录进行的,调整分录有助于达到权责发生制会计的目标:在实现收入时确认收入;在相关的商品和劳务使用时确认费用。每当经济业务对收入和费用的影响超过一个会计期间时,都需要通过调整分录进行调账。

2. adjusting entries 调整分录,包括摊配已入账(会计)记录的调整分录(Adjusting Entries Covering Recorded Data),比如说预付保险费(Prepaid Insurance)、预付房租费(Prepaid Rent)、库存物料(Supplies on Hand)、累计折旧(accumulated depreciation)、备抵坏账(即坏账准备 Allowance for Uncollectible Accounts)等;还包括未入账(会计)记录的调整分录(记提未记录的费用 Adjusting Entries Covering Unrecorded Data),比如说部分跨期工资费用(Accrued Salaries)等。

3. an accrual basis of accounting 应计基础或权责发生制,是以应收应付作为标准来处理经济业务、确定本期收入和费用来计算本期盈亏的会计处理基础。在应计基础上，凡属本期已经获得的收入、已经收到的现款均作为本期的收入（revenue is recognized when it is earned, regardless of when cash is actually collected）；凡属本期应负担的费用，不管是否付出现款都作为本期的费用处理（expense is matched to the revenue, regardless of when cash is paid out）。当我们提供了某项商品或者服务之后，就视为取得了收益，因为此时商品和服务的所有权已经发生了转移，而这已经产生了付款的法定义务（At this time, title to the goods or services is transferred, and there is created a legal obligation to pay for such goods or services）。应计基础作为流行的会计惯例，尽管比较麻烦，但是因为它能正确计算盈亏，所以一般企业都采用应计制，除非一些较小的企业（Accounting records are kept on an accrual basis, except in the case of very small businesses）。

4. a cash basis of accounting 现金收付基础或收付实现制，是以款项的实际收付为标准来处理经济业务，确定本期的收入和费用，计算本期盈亏的会计处理基础。它和应计制一起成为现代会计中确定收入和费用的两大基础。在现金收付基础上，凡是在本期以现款付出的费用，不论其应否在本期收入中获得补偿均应作为本期费用处理；凡是在本期实际收到的现款收入，不论其是否属于本期均应作为本期收入处理。这种处理方法的好处是计算简单，符合心理习惯，但是按照这种方法计算的盈亏不合理、不准确，所以一般企业不采用，只是在某些个体工商户和小企业中采用。

5. This account is known as a contra asset (which has the opposite balance of its asset), and it summarizes and accumulates the amount of depreciation over the equipment's total useful life.

此类账户被称为备抵账户（借贷方向与其相对应的资产类账户相反），备抵账户总结和累计了设备等大型固定资产整个使用周期全部的折旧。

6. Allowance for Uncollectible Accounts 备抵坏账，即坏账准备或坏账损失。坏账损失的估计数一般可以过去的经验为基础，并适当考虑销售业务的预测。会计上在计算应收账款可能发生的无法收回情况（即坏账损失）时，先将可能发生的坏账损失数记入"备抵坏账"科目贷方，同时借记"管理费用——坏账损失"科目；当该笔应收账款确定无法收回时，再借记"备抵坏账"科目，同时贷记"应收账款"科目。

7. Accounting records are kept on an accrual basis, except in the case of very small businesses. To accrue means to collect or accumulate. This means that revenue is recognized when it is earned, regardless of when cash is actually collected, and expense is matched to the revenue, regardless of when cash is paid out.

除了一些很小的企业，会计记录都是在应计制（即权责发生制）的基础上进行的。"应计"意味着要（及时）归集和累计（各种收入和费用），也意味着不管现金什么时候收到，收入都要在实现时及时予以确认；并且不管现金何时付出，费用都要与收入相配比（即任何费用都应该是由某项收入引起的），且与相配比的收入同时入账。

8. Some revenue, such as rental income, is recognized on a time basis and is earned when the specified period of time has passed. The accrual concept demands that expenses be kept in step with revenue, so that each month sees only that month's expenses applied against the revenue for that month.

某些收入，例如租金收入，是在期间基础（即应计制或称权责发生制）上予以确认的，但其现金流入却是在其被确认为收入的那个具体期间已经过去之后（例如，出租给别人的房屋，六月份的租金收入应在当月就予以确认,但租金却可能到七月份或八月份才收到)。应计制要求费用支出一定要与其相配比的收入同步入账,所以每月确认的费用只能是与当月收入相关的各项支出。

9. Assume that a business paid a $1,200 premium on April 1 for one year's insurance in advance.

假设某公司于 4 月 1 日预付了其后一年的保险费共 1200 美元(此处的 for one year 表明其支付的是从当天算起一整年的费用,即从 4 月 1 日到第二年的 3 月 31 日)。

10. Assume that on March 1 a business paid $1,500 to cover rent for the balance of the year.

假设某公司在 3 月 1 日预付了当年剩余月份的全部租金共 1500 美元(此处的 for the balance of the year 表明其支付的是从当天算起到当年结束的费用,即从 3 月 1 日到 12 月 31 日)。

11. the straight-line method of accounting　直线法。这是会计上计提折旧的一种方法,这种方法是通过将某项固定资产的原值 original (historical) cost 减去预计净残值,再除以该固定资产的预计使用期限(life expectancy)来确定每年计提的折旧额,在直线法下,每年计提的折旧额都是一样的,故该方法的计算及会计处理都较为简单。

12. matching　配比。根据配比原则,为赚取收入而发生的费用应当在确认收入实现的期间予以确认。

5.2　Adjusting Entries Covering Unrecorded Data
(对未入账的(会计)记录的调整分录)

Adjusting Entries Covering Unrecorded Data

In the previous section, we discussed various kinds of adjustments to accounts to which entries had already been made. Now we consider those instances in which an expense has been incurred. For example, if salaries are paid on a weekly basis, the last week of the month may apply to 2 months. If April ends on a Tuesday, then the first 2 days of the week will apply to April and be an April expense, while the last 3 days will be a May expense. To arrive at the proper total for salaries for the month of April, we must include, along with the April payrolls that were paid in April, the 2 days' salary that was not paid until May. Thus, we make an entry to accrue the 2 days' salary. As mentioned earlier, to accrue means to collect or accumulate.

The following example shows an adjusting entry for the most common type of unrecorded expenses (accrued expenses).

Examples

Accrued Salaries

Assume that April 30 falls on Tuesday for the last weekly payroll period. Then, 2 days of that week will apply to April and 3 days to May. The payroll is $500 per day, for the week, or $2,500. For this example, $1,000 would apply to April (Monday and Tuesday) and $1,500 to

May (Wednesday, Thursday, and Friday).

April 29	April 30	May 1	May 2	May 3
Monday	Tuesday	Wednesday	Thursday	Friday
$500	$500	$500	$500	$500

The entries would be as follows:

    Apr. 30   Salaries Expense   1,000
                Salaries Payable   1,000

When the payment of the payroll is made—say, on May 3—the entry would be as follows:

    May 3   Salaries Expense   1,500
             Salaries Payable   1,000
             Cash   2,500

As can be seen, $1,000 was charged to expense in April and $1,500 in May. The debit to Salaries Payable of $1,000 in May merely canceled the credit entry made in April, when the liability was set up for the April salaries expense.

 New Words, Phrases and Special Terms

accrued expenses		应计费用
accrued salaries		应计工资，薪金
along with		按照，循着，根据
apply to		运用，应用，适用
entry	n.	记载，记录
fall on		处于，处在
instance	n.	例子
incur	vt.	招致，发生
payroll	n.	工资（册、表）
salary	n.	薪水，奖金
salaries expense		工资费用
salaries payable		应付工资
say	v.	假设，比方说
unrecorded	adj.	未记录的，未登记的

Notes

1. For example, if salaries are paid on a weekly basis, the last week of the month may apply to 2 months.

比方说，如果工资薪水是在周薪基础（每周一次）上支付的，那么每月最后一周的薪水在会计记录上可能会横跨两个月。

2. If April ends on a Tuesday, then the first 2 days of the week will apply to April and be an April expense, while the last 3 days will be a May expense.

如果四月份终结于星期二，那么那一周的前两天适用于四月份，即记作四月份的费用，而后三天记作五月份的费用。

3. To arrive at the proper total for salaries for the month of April, we must include, along with the April payrolls that were paid in April, the 2 days' salary that was not paid until May.

要正确地合计四月份的薪资总额，我们须按照四月份的薪资表计算出当月支付的薪资和五月份才支出的最后两天薪资。

5.3　Closing Entries
（结账分录）

Closing Entries

After the income statement and balance sheet have been prepared, a summary account variously known as Expense and Income Summary, Profit and Loss Summary, and so on is set up. Then, by means of closing entries, each expense account is credited so as to produce a zero balance, and the total amount for the closed-out accounts is debited to Expense and Income Summary. Similarly, the individual revenue accounts are closed out by debiting, and the total amount is credited to the summary account. Thus, the new fiscal year starts with zero balances in the income and expense accounts, whereas the Expense and Income Summary balance gives the net income or the net loss for the old year.

Examples

To illustrate the closing procedure, we refer to the accounts of T. Drew.

T. Drew
Trial Balance
January 31, 200X

Cash	$3,900
Supplies	100

Furniture	2,000	
Accounts Payable		$800
T. Drew, Capital		4,000
T. Drew, Drawing	400	
Fees Income		2,500
Rent Expense	500	
Salaries Expense	200	
Supplies Expense	200	
	$7,300	$7,300

The closing entries are as follows:

(1) Close out income accounts. Debit the individual income accounts and credit the total to Expense and Income Summary. Here, there is only one income account.

    Jan. 31 Fees Income   2,500
          Expense and Income Summary 2,500

(2) Close out expense accounts. Credit the individual expense accounts and debit the total to Expense and Income Summary.

    Jan. 31 Expense and Income Summary 900
          Rent Expense   500
         Salaries Expense   200
         Supplies Expense   200

(3) Close out the Expense and Income Summary account. If there is a profit, the credit made for total income in (1) above will exceed the debit made for total expense in (2) above. Therefore, to close out the balance to zero, a debit entry will be made to Expense and Income Summary. A credit will be made to the capital account to transfer the net income for the period. If expenses exceed income, then a loss has been sustained, and a credit is made to Expense and Income Summary and a debit to the capital account. Based on the information given, the entry is:

    Jan. 31 Expense and Income Summary 1,600
         T. Drew, Capital   1,600

(4) Close out the Drawing account. The drawing account would be credited for the total amount of the drawings for the period and the capital account would be debited for that amount. The difference between net income and drawing for the period represents the net change in the capital account for the period. The net income of $1,600, less drawings of $400, results in a net increase of $1,200 in the capital account. The closing entry for the drawing account is:

    Jan. 31 T. Drew, Capital   400
         T. Drew, Drawing   400

In summary, the procedure is as follows:

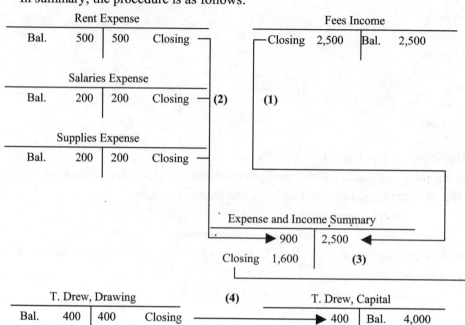

After the closing entries (1) through (4) are made,
(1) Close Fees Income account to Expense and Income Summary
(2) Close all expense accounts to Expense and Income Summary
(3) Close Expense and Income Summary to the Capital account
(4) Close the Drawing account to the Capital account

the various accounts will appear as shown. The income and expense accounts and the drawing account are ruled off or closed out, thus showing no balance. The net profit for the period and the drawing account balance were transferred to T. Drew, Capital, a balance sheet account.

Cash		Furniture		T. Drew, Capital	
Bal. 3,900		Bal. 2,000		(4) 400	Bal. 4,000
					1,600 (3)

Supplies		Accounts Payable		T. Drew, Drawing	
Bal. 100			Bal. 800	Bal. 400	400 (4)

Fees Income				Salaries Expense				Expense and Income Summary			
(1)	2,500	Bal.	2,500	Bal.	200	200	(2)	(2)	900	2,500	(1)
								(3)	1,600		
									2,500	2,500	

Rent Expense				Supplies Expense			
Bal.	500	500	(2)	Bal.	200	200	(2)

Note: The above transactions are based on the sole proprietorship form of business. If this business were a corporation, the Capital account would be replaced by the Retained Earnings account.

New Words, Phrases and Special Terms

by means of		通过，用，凭借
close accounts		结清账户
close out		结清（账户余额）
drawing account		（业主）提款账户
expense and income summary		损益汇总
profit and loss summary		收益或亏损汇总（本年利润）
rule off		划线隔开以便于结清（账户余额）
retained earnings account		留存收益（账户名）
sustain	vt.	证明，确定
set up		建立，创立，树立
variously	adv.	各式各样地

 Notes

1. After the income statement and balance sheet have been prepared, a summary account variously known as Expense and Income Summary, Profit and Loss Summary, and so on is setup.

在损益表及资产负债表填制好以后，需要开设一个总结性科目称为"本年利润"账户以总结当年的费用及收入、利润或损失。

2. Then, by means of closing entries, each expense account is credited so as to produce a zero balance, and the total amount for the closed-out accounts is debited to Expense and Income Summary.

通过结账分录，所有的费用支出类账户应该全部贷记以使账户余额为零，同时将所有已结清的（费用类账户）余额借记损益汇总账户。

3. Thus, the new fiscal year starts with zero balances in the income and expense accounts, whereas the Expense and Income Summary balance gives the net income or the net loss for the old year.

这样从新财务年度开始起就没有收入和费用账户余额（余额为零），同时本年利润账户期初余额表示的是上一年实现的净利润或净亏损。

4. closing 结账。收入和费用账户是暂记性质的资本类账户，用于在会计期内分类和汇总对业主权益产生影响的某些变化。在会计期末，要把这些各种各样的增减变化的最终结果转入业主资本账户，同时将这些暂记性质的资本类账户的余额降为零，以使这些账户更好地衡量下个会计期间的收入与费用。这个转账的过程就称为结账，结账一般是通过编制结账分录（Closing Entry）进行的。包括，结清营业收入账户（Close out Income Accounts）、结清费用账户（Close out Expense Accounts）、结清收益总额（Close out the Expense and Income Summary Account）、结清业主提款账户（Close out the Drawing Account）。即：

(1) Close Fees Income Account to Expense and Income Summary 将收入类账户结转到收益费用汇总账户，结清收入账户。

(2) Close all Expense Accounts to Expense and Income Summary 将费用类账户结转到收益费用汇总账户，结清费用账户。

(3) Close Expense and Income Summary to the Capital account 将收益费用汇总账户余额转入资本（业主权益）账户，结清收益费用汇总账户。

(4) Close the Drawing account to the Capital account 将业主提款账户余额转入资本（业主权益）账户，结清业主提款账户。

5.4 Ruling Accounts
（账户的划线结清）

Ruling Accounts

After the posting of the closing entries, all revenue and expense accounts and the summary accounts are closed. When ruling an account where only one debit and one credit exist, a double rule is drawn below the entry across the debit and credit money columns. The date and reference columns also have a double rule, in order to separate the transactions from the period just ended and the entry to be made in the subsequent period.

Examples

1.

Salaries Expense

Date	Item	P.R.	Debit	Date	Item	P.R.	Credit
Jan. 30		J-1	200	Jan. 31		J-2	200

If more than one entry appears on either side of the account, a single ruled line is drawn

Chapter 5 Adjusting and Closing Procedures（调账和结账）

below the last entry across the debit and credit money columns. The totals are entered just below the single line, and a double ruling line is drawn below the totals. The date and reference column also will have a double ruling line.

2.

Expense and Income Summary

Date	Item	P.R.	Debit	Date	Item	P.R.	Credit
Jan. 31		J-2	900	Jan. 31		J-1	2,500
31		J-2	1,600				
			2,500				2,500

The assets, liabilities, and capital accounts will have balances. These open accounts are ruled so that their balances are carried forward to the new fiscal year.

3.

Cash

Date	Item	P.R.	Debit	Date	Item	P.R.	Credit
Jan. 4			4,000	Jan. 4			300
15			2,500	30			500
				30			200
				31			1,200
	3,900			31			400
			6,500				2,600
					Bal.		
			6,500				3,900
							6,500
Feb. 1	Bal.		3,900				

Balance of the account. Pencil footing → 3,900

The balance of the account is entered on the first day of the following month.

Note: When there are several entries on each side, both the debit column and the credit column are pencil-footed. The pencil footing of one side is subtracted from the other side. The difference is written in the "Item" column on the side of the account that has the larger total.

5.5 Post-Closing Trial Balance
（结账后试算平衡表）

Post-Closing Trial Balance

After the closing entries have been made and the accounts ruled, only balance sheet accounts assets, liabilities, and capital remain open. It is desirable to produce another trial balance to ensure that the accounts are in balance. This is known as a ***post-closing trial balance***.

Examples

T. Drew

Post-Closing Trial Balance

January 31, 200X

Cash	$3,900	
Supplies	100	
Furniture	2,000	
Accounts Payable		$800
T. Drew, Capital		5,200
	$6,000	$6,000

 New Words, Phrases and Special Terms

a double ruled (ruling) line		双线标志
a single ruled line		一条单线
carry forward		结转
column	n.	专栏
desirable	adj.	需要的，可取的
corporation	n.	公司
open account		未结清的账户
pencil-footed	adj.	用铅笔注脚的
post-closing trial balance		结账后试算（平衡）表
ruling	n.	划线
retained earnings account		未分配利润账户
subtract	v.	减，作减法
subsequent	adj.	后来的，附随的，其后的

trial balance 试算平衡表

 Notes

1. When ruling an account where only one debit and one credit exist, a double rule is drawn below the entry across the debit and credit money columns.

当结清那些只有借方或贷方余额的账户时,应该在借贷余额下面划双线。

2. The date and reference columns also have a double rule, in order to separate the transactions from the period just ended and the entry to be made in the subsequent period.

日期及附注栏也有双线标志,目的是将该项交易在已结束的会计期间与下一会计期间区分清楚。

3. After the closing entries have been made and the accounts ruled, only balance sheet accounts assets, liabilities, and capital remain open. It is desirable to produce another trial balance to ensure that the accounts are in balance.

在结账分录完成并用双划线隔开标明之后,仅有资产负债表中的资产、负债及所有者权益类账户仍未结清(有余额),此时需要进行一次试算平衡以确定这些账户余额相互之间是否平衡。

4. post-closing trial balance 结账后试算平衡表。结账分录做完后,为了避免结账中出现的错误,会计上要求再作一次试算平衡以验证资产负债表左边的资产类科目合计数与右边的负债及所有者权益类科目合计数是否相等,为编制会计报表做好充分的准备。

 Section II　Review & Exercises（复习与练习）

 **Summary**

1. The basis of accounting that recognizes revenue when it is earned, regardless of when cash is received, and matches the expenses to the revenue, regardless of when cash is paid out, is known as the _____.

2. An adjusting entry that records the expired amount of prepaid insurance would create the _____ account.

3. Supplies on hand is classified as an _____ and appears in the _____, whereas supplies expense is an _____ and appears in the _____.

4. Accrued salaries is treated in the balance sheet as a _____, whereas Salaries Expense appears in the income statement as an _____.

5. Both Allowance for Uncollectible Accounts and Accumulated Depreciation appear in the balance sheet as _____ from their related assets.

6. The related accounts discussed in Question 5 are _____ and _____.
7. An expense paid in advance is known as a _____.
8. The revenue and expense accounts are closed out to the summary account known as _____.
9. Eventually, all income, expense, and drawing accounts, including summaries, are closed into the _____ account.
10. The post-closing trial balance involves only _____, _____, and _____ accounts.

Questions

1. What is posting?
2. What is closing?
3. How to describe an accounting cycle?
4. How to understand the accrual basis and the cash basis of accounting?
5. What is the straight-line method of accounting?
6. How to understand the expense should be matched to the revenue?

Solved Problems

1. A business pays weekly salaries of $10,000 on Friday for the 5-day week. Show the adjusting entry when the fiscal period ends on (1) Tuesday; (2) Thursday.

(1)				
(2)				

2. An insurance policy covering a 2-year period was purchased on November 1 for $600. The amount was debited to Prepaid Insurance. Show the adjusting entry for the 2-month period ending December 31.

3. Office supplies purchases of $900 were debited to Office Supplies. A count of the supplies at end of the period showed $500 on hand. Make the adjusting entry at the end of the

period.

4. Machinery costing $12,000, purchased November 30, is being depreciated at the rate of 10 percent per year. Show the adjusting entry for December 31.

5. A large tractor (拖拉机,牵引机) costing $60,000 was purchased on September 30, is being depreciated by the straight-line method over 5 years, and has no salvage(剩余的,残余的) value. Show the year-end adjusting entry. (The tractor was put into use on October 1.)

6. Salaries paid to employees are $500 per day. The weekly payroll ends on Friday, but Tuesday is the last day of the accounting period. Show the necessary adjusting entry (5-day week).

7. On June 1, Dry Lake camps purchased a 3-year fire insurance policy costing $9,000. This was debited to a Prepaid Insurance account. The camp's year ends on November 30.

(1) Show the necessary adjusting entry. (2) Show the entry if the above insurance policy was debited to an Insurance Expense account.

(1)

(2)

8. Supplies costing $2,000 were debited to Supplies. The year-end inventory showed $1,150 of supplies on hand. (1) Show the necessary year-end adjusting entry. (2) Show the above

adjusting entry if the supplies were debited to a Supplies Expense account when purchased.

(1)

(2)

9. (1) The balance in the Prepaid Insurance account, before adjustments, is $1,800, and the amount expired during the year is $1,200. The amount needed for the adjusting entry required is _____.

(2) A business pays weekly salaries (5-day week) of $4,000 on Friday. The amount of the adjusting entry necessary at the end of the fiscal period ending on Wednesday is _____.

(3) On December 31, the end of the fiscal year, the supplies account had a balance before adjustment of $650. The fiscal supply inventory account on December 31 is $170. The amount of the adjusting entry is _____.

(4) The supplies account on December 31 has an inventory of $500. The supplies used during the year is $200. The amount of the adjusting entry to record this information is _____.

10. Listed are the T accounts of Douglas Money, financial advisor. The year-end adjustment necessary to bring the accounts up to date are as follows:

(1) Inventory of supplies at end of year was $395.
(2) Depreciation for the year was $900.
(3) Wages owed but not paid were $725.
(4) Utilities owed but not paid were $215.
(5) Insurance expense for the year was $1,150.
(6) Cash sales not yet posted were $2,175.

Cash	Accounts Receivable	Supplies	D. Money, Drawing
7,555	1,750	915	1,250

Chapter 5 Adjusting and Closing Procedures（调账和结账）

Accounts Payable	D. Money, Capital	Wages Expense
975	17,000	20,665

Prepaid Insurance	Fees Income	Utilities Expense
1,575	16,450	715

First, prepare the adjusting journal entries. Then, make the necessary adjustments to the T accounts.

Adjusting Entries

(1)

(2)

(3)

(4)

(5)

(6)

Cash	Accounts Receivable	Supplies	Accounts Payable
7,555	1,750	915	975

D. Money, Capital	Wages Expense	Prepaid Insurance	Fees Income
17,000	20,665	1,575	16,450

Utilities Expense	Supplies Expense	Depreciation Expense	Accumulated Depreciation
715			

Wages Payable	Insurance Expense	D. Money, Drawing

11. From the preceding problem about Douglas Money, prepare the closing entries from the T accounts after you made the necessary adjustments.

Closing Entries

(1)			
(2)			
(3)			
(4)			

12. Prior to the adjustment on December 31, the Salaries Expense account had a debit of $200,000. Salaries owed, but not yet paid, totaled $5,000. Present the entries required to record the following:

(1) Accrued salary as of December 31.
(2) The closing of the salary expense account.

(1)			

			(continued)
(2)			

13. Selected accounts from the ledger are presented in T-account form below. Journalize the adjusting entries that have been posted to the accounts.

Cash		Salaries Payable	
36,860			4,000

Prepaid Insurance		Capital	
600	200		32,000

Supplies		Expense and Income Summary	
540	240		

Equipment		Fees Income	
6,000			12,000

Accumulated Depreciation		Salaries Expense	
	1,800	4,000	

		Insurance Expense	
		200	

		Depreciation Expense	
		1,800	

		Supplies Expense	
		240	

		(continued)

14. From the information in Problem 13, present the necessary closing entries.

(1)			
(2)			
(3)			

15. Form the information in Problem 14, prepare a post-closing trial balance.

Account	Dr.	Cr.

16. The trial balance before closing shows service income of $10,000 and interest income of $2,000. The expenses are: salaries, $6,000; rent, $2,000; depreciation, $1,500; and interest, $500. Give the closing entries to be made to Expense and Income Summary for (1) income and (2)

expenses.

(1)			
(2)			

17. Using the solution to Problem 16, prepare the closing entry for net income, and post the transactions to the Expense and Income Summary and to the capital account, which had a prior balance of $20,000. Finally, close out the applicable account.


```
     Expense and Income Summary                Capital
   (2)  10,000  |  12,000  (1)              Bal. | 20,000
   (3)    ?     |                                |
```

18. After all revenue and expense accounts were closed at the end of the fiscal year, the Expense and Income Summary had a debit total of $100,000 and a credit total of $150,000. The capital account for Laura Anthony had a credit balance of $50,000; and Laura Anthony, Drawing, had a debit balance of $35,000. Journalize the closing entries.

19. Based on the balances below, prepare entries to close out (1) income accounts, (2) expense accounts, (3) Expense and Income Summary, (4) drawing account.

P. Silvergold, Capital		$22,000
P. Silvergold, Drawing	$6,000	
Service Income		12,000

Interest Income		1,500
Wages and Salaries Expense	8,000	
Rent Expense	4,000	
Depreciation Expense	3,000	
Interest Expense	2,000	

(1)

(2)

(3)

(4)

Section III Reading Material（阅读材料）

Accrual Basis Accounting and Cash Basis Accounting

In firms that employ *an basis accounting system*（权责发生制）revenue is recognized when earned rather than when cash is collected and expenses are recognized when goods and services are used rather than when they are paid for. The expenses incurred are matched with the relative revenue earned in order to determine a meaningful net income figure for each accounting period. Yet, certain businesses, principally *service enterprises*（服务业企业）, often use a *cash basis*（收付实现制）mode of accounting. In contrast to accrual basis accounting, the cash basis system does recognize revenues when money is received and expenses when money is paid. Cash basis accounting is used primarily because it can provide certain income tax benefits and because it is simple. However, cash basis financial statements may *distort*（歪曲，曲解）the *portrayal*（记述，描绘）of financial position and operating results of a business because the revenue and expenses for determining net income do not depend on the time period when cash is actually received or expended. *Consequently*（因此，结果）, most business firms use the accrual basis of accounting.

 Answer the following questions:

1. Why is the adjusting step of the accounting cycle necessary?
2. What four different types of adjustments are frequently needed at the end of an accountting period?
3. Give examples for each of the four types of adjustments.
4. How do the accrual basis and the cash basis of accounting differ?

Chapter 6   Review: Financial Awareness
（复习：财务意识）

导学：本章将讨论公司财务中所要面对的基本财会问题，介绍各种财务文件，并讲解创立企业所需要准备的创业计划。

 Section I   Accounting Study（会计学习）

Finance is important for all managers in the business world today, and in this chapter you can look at the words needed to communicate effectively in English about financial matters. You'll study the basic terms used in the most common financial statements used by companies and other organizations, and you will study the importance of cash flow for all businesses and you will look at what can go wrong without good financial management. At the end of the chapter you willl study a report about a company's finances and write your own report about debtors.

6.1   Financial Documents
（财务文件）

Alan Parkinson, from Suzhou Economy &Trade Institute, describes the purpose of each of the main financial statements used by British companies: the annual report, the balance sheet, the profit and loss account and the cash-flow forecast.

One of the challenges that all organizations have is being able to account for the flow of finance which comes into it, as an organization, and then goes out of it and also, of course, what happens in between coming in and going out.

Most organizations will prepare a number of financial reports. One of the most common is the annual report, and it will look back over the year and will talk about the profit and loss account, detail the cash-flow forecast, where cash has come from, where it's gone, and also will look at the balance sheet at the start of the year that's just ended, and also the balance sheet at the end of the year.

And in most countries where there is a developed accounting system, particularly in continental and Western Europe, what you'll find is that there is a statutory obligation for companies who have shareholders to report back to the shareholders as to what has happened to the business over the year.

The profit and loss account is nothing more than saying "let's look at the cost of the outputs that we achieved during the year, and let's match that against the sales, take the difference and give us the profit". The balance sheet is saying "let's list, at any moment in time, what the sources of finance are, so, from shareholders, from banks and as we now know, from reinvested profits, and let's list down where that financing has gone—has it been spent on cars, has it been spent on equipment, has it been spent on offices, on materials, is there some cash left over which is just sitting there?" So the balance sheet just becomes a statement of the sources of finance and the resources that finance has been expended upon.

 New Words, Phrases and Special Terms

account for		说明，解释
analyse	vt. n.	分析
annual report		年度报告
awareness	n.	意识
cash flow		现金流
consequences	n.	结果，后果
continental	adj.	大陆的，欧洲大陆的，美洲的
day-to-day	adj.	日常的
detail	vt. n.	详述，细节
dominate	v.	支配
financial	adj.	财务的，财政的，金融的
forecast	vt. n.	预报，预测
look back		回顾
obligation	n.	义务
profit and loss account		损益账户
reinvested profits		净利润再投资
revise	vt.	修订
statutory	adj.	法定的
trend	n.	趋势

6.2　Cash-Flow Problems
（现金流问题）

In this passage you will look at the importance of cash flow and the reasons for business failure.

There are many reasons why companies fail but cash-flow problems and over-trading are often weak spots. New companies often find that they have too much money tied up in the business and so find themselves in debt and, eventually, they run out of money and their creditors take them to court to have them wound up. The company then goes out of business.

Kenny Chan found there was a lack of good bicycle shops in his part of Sydney, so he decided to open one. He managed to borrow enough money from the bank to open Supercycles. Before opening the shop, Kenny bought a large stock of different types of bicycles and paid cash for them. After his first day in business, Kenny felt that he had indeed found a gap in the market. He had quickly sold five mountain bikes for $500 each, double what he had paid. However, only one of his customers had paid cash. After six months in business, Kenny realized that most bicycles spent a month in his shop before being sold and customers took an average of 60 days to pay him. This meant that three months passed between him paying for the bicycle and his customer paying him. Kenny had a lot of customers but he had to borrow more money from the bank in order to buy new stock. He also found that mountain bikes were selling well but ladies' bikes were not, And he had too many in stock. He also had a large number of bicycle accessories that were not selling well and his suppliers were demanding payment. After a year in business, Kenny's order books were full but he could not afford to buy any more stock for his shop and the money he made in sales didn't cover the interest to the bank. Soon the banks demanded repayment, he couldn't buy any more stock because he didn't have any cash so customers went to other shops, and his suppliers took him to court because he hadn't paid them. In less than two years Supercycles had gone out of business.

6.3　Collecting Overdue Account Letters
（催收账款信函）

The letter below is from one of Super cycle's suppliers reminding Kenny Chan to pay an outstanding invoice.

Chapter 6 Review: Financial Awareness (复习：财务意识)

```
                                      15 Somerset Road
                   RTX                Bristol
                                      BR22 3SE
                   PLC                United Kingdom
                                      3 June 2000

Ref: 12/ABD/34

Mr. Kenney Chan
Supercycles
13 Friday lane
Sydney
NSW 2010
Australia
Dear Mr. Chan
Re: Invoice No.UN135X
```

We notice from our records that the above invoice, which was sent to you on 1 April, has not yet been paid.

As specified on the invoice, our terms of payment are 30-day net. Your invoice has now been outstanding for 60 days.

We would appreciate it if you could either let us have your remittance within the next ten days or send us an explanation of why the invoice is still outstanding. I enclose a copy of the original invoice in case you have mislaid it.

We look forward to receiving your payment.
Yours sincerely
Alanna foster
  Accountant
Enc: Invoice No.UN135X

The letter above is a typical business letter. Notice the following points.

- The addresses

The sender's address is usually in the top right corner and the address of the person or organization to whom the letter is being sent is below it and on the left. In the UK the building number is put first, followed by the street and then the city or town. Nowadays, it is common not to have any commas in the address. If commas are omitted from the address, they should also be omitted after "Dear Sir/Madam" etc, and "Yours faithfully/sincerely".

- The date

The date usually appears under the sender's address, but it can be put above the address of the person or organization to whom the letter is being sent. It can be written in several different ways; the most common is "29 February 2000", but this could also be written as 29/2/2000.It is important to remember that in some countries, including the USA, the day and the month would be reversed, i.e.2/29/2000.

- Opening and closing

If you begin a letter "Dear Mr. Brown" you should finish it "Yours sincerely", but if you don't know the name of the person you are writing to, you should begin the letter with "Dear sir", "Dear Madam", "Dear Sir/Madam" or "Dear Madam/Sir" and finish it "Yours faithfully".

- The subject

It isn't necessary to include a subject line to say what the letter is about, but if you do it should be written below the opening "Dear…" and underlined or made italic. This is often introduced with "Re:", which means "about".

- Reference

"Ref:" is used when a reference is given to a particular file or case; it will look something like "Ref: 12/ABD/34". Such references are usually given at the top of the letter, either under the sender's address or above the address of the person or organization to whom the letter is being sent.

- Signature, name and title

You should sign the letter under "Yours sincerely/faithfully" and then put your full name and job title under your signature. In the UK your name is not written with the address at the top of the letter as it is in some other countries.

- Enclosures

If you are enclosing something with your letter, you can use the abbreviation "Enc" below your name and title, followed by details of what is enclosed.

Because very few persons or firms pay for their purchases as they make them, they accumulate debts. If these debts are not paid when they are due, letters are written to ask these people for payment. Often a series of letters is necessary to get customers or clients to pay. Many firms have a time schedule for sending such letters. The first letter is sent when the account is delinquent for a certain period of time; the second, so many days later; and so forth.

Collection letters have two purposes: first, to collect the past-due account and, second, to keep the customer's goodwill. Even if a firm successfully collects its past-due accounts, it needs to keep the customer buying from the firm. It cannot operate without repeat business; therefore, a firm cannot afford to antagonize its customers.

Descriptions of the various steps in collecting overdue accounts are given here. However, different firms follow different collection policies and procedures. For example, some are more lenient, while others speed the process by writing fewer letters.

First Reminder

The first notification in collecting overdue accounts is generally a reminder. It can be as simple as a rubber stamp or a printed notice or a gummed sticker over the statement; it is usually not a letter. If it is a computer billing, the machine has been programmed to add a line telling the customer that the account is overdue. You are assuming that the obligation has been overlooked; therefore, you are sending a reminder. Writing a collection letter at this point would risk losing the customer's goodwill and also incur the expense of writing the letter.

Second Communication

The second step in the collection series is a letter written to ask why the company has not been paid. You assume that there is a reason for not paying and that something is wrong. The letter should have a helpful tone. Every attempt should be made to make it easy for the customer to pay—enclose a return envelope or ask the customer to call or to communicate in some way.

Example 1

The opening reviews the situation:

We have not received the December payment of $44 that was due on your television set, and it will soon be time for the January payment.

The body begins with an offer of help and then explains what is wanted. The closing is a courteous goodbye:

Because you have met previous payments promptly, we think something must have happened that has prevented you from making the December payment. If so, can we help in some way?

Would you please send us your check for $44? You may also include the January payment by sending your check for $88. If you cannot pay the entire amount at this time, would you please explain your difficulty to us and let us know your plans for making these payments.

Should your check already be in the mail, please accept our thanks.

In this collection letter, do not suggest reasons for the nonpayment, such as that the statement did not arrive or that it was overlooked in the rush of Christmas holidays. Too, do not suggest that the product or services were unsatisfactory; if they were, the customer would have complained before the account became past-due. Let the customer explain the nonpayment for you.

Third Communication

The next letter in the series will be stronger. It will attempt to get the customer to pay by appealing to such things as sense of fair play, desire for a good reputation or credit standing, or security. You are not offering in this letter to help; you want the bill paid.

This is an example of an appeal to maintaining a good credit standing:

We wrote you three weeks ago asking that you send us your check for $88 to cover the December and January payments on your television set. We have not heard from you.

Because you have always made your payments promptly, you have a fine credit standing with our company. We are sure that you wish to maintain this rating. Therefore, won't you please send us your check within next five days?

Use the enclosed envelope for your check. When we receive your payment, your credit rating will again be rated highly.

Fourth Communication

If appealing to the customer brings no response, usually one more letter is written before the threatening, last-chance letter. This letter is more demanding; every effort is used, however, to avoid the final threat.

Example 2

We are sure that you have received our previous letters asking for payment of your delinquent account. We know that your credit rating is excellent, as we made a routine check before extending credit to you.

Now that credit rating is threatened by your not paying our account, which amounts to $132. If this amount is not paid, the resulting loss of your good credit rating will restrict further credit purchases and force you into the inconvenience of paying cash for all of your purchases.

Because your account is so long overdue, we must ask our Legal Department to take over. Should this happen, there will be additional legal costs.

We will not turn this account over to our Legal Department for seven days, for we are sure that your check will be here before that time. The enclosed envelope is directed to my desk for immediate attention. Please use it to send us your check.

Final Communication

When none of the previous appeals has produced payment, the last letter is "pay now or face legal action". Building goodwill is no longer an important consideration; you would like to keep the customer's business, but you want to collect what is owed. There should be no abusive or angry language, but the tone of the letter should be strong, firm, and clear.

The final letter should review what you have done in an attempt to collect the account. It should tell what effect nonpayment, will have on the customer's credit standing, and it should state precisely the steps that you will take if the account is not paid.

Example 3

We have written you four times over the past three months in our efforts to collect $132 that is now six months past-due.

As you have not replied to any of our reminders or letters asking for payment, we are forced to take legal steps to collect this overdue account. Are you aware what this will do to your credit standing? We must, when we take legal action to collect any account, notify the credit bureau of our action. They, in turn, will change your credit rating accordingly.

Therefore, unless we receive your check for $132 by May 1, we will notify our Legal Department to proceed with a suit to collect this amount. If this involves court action, costs will be added.

We hope that you will not force us to take this unpleasant action.

Using Special Postal Services

Using some of the special postal services is sometimes effective in collecting slow-paying accounts. The importance of the letter can be emphasized by sending it by certified mail with or without a requested return receipt. A return receipt furnishes proof that the letter was actually received. You can, too, for payment of an additional fee, restrict delivery to the addressee. The cost of sending telegrams to collect overdue accounts makes it impractical in most instances.

Form Collection

Often firms compose a series of form collection letters. Sometimes these letters are programmed into the computer. At certain predetermined intervals, the computer writes letters to customers with overdue accounts. This can antagonize because, not only is the appearance of the letter usually mechanical and impersonal, but the computer does not take into consideration any replies that the customer may have written. In addition, the computer can send collection letters to persons who either do not actually owe the debt or who, because of a question concerning the account, are withholding payment of the bill.

Duplicated Collection Letters

Collection letters with names and amounts added to duplicated forms are impersonal. Therefore, they are more likely to be disregarded. They might be effective, though, as first reminders because they are so impersonal and would, as they are intended to do, gently remind customers of overdue accounts.

New Words, Phrases and Special Terms

abbreviation	n.	缩写
abusive	adj.	辱骂的，滥用的
accessory	n..	附件，零件，配件
addressee	n.	收信人
antagonize	vt.	使敌对，使反感
appropriately	adv.	适合地
autonomous	adj.	自治的
client	n.	客户
conscientiously	adj.	细心的，谨慎从事的
courteous	adj.	礼貌的
credit standing		信誉
delinquent	adj.	拖欠（债务）的
disregard	v. n.	不尊重
donate	v.	捐赠
duplicated	adj.	复制的，复写的
enclose	vt.	装入信封
enclosure	n.	信中附件
entrust	v.	委托
go out of business		破产
inconvenience	n.	不方便
italic	adj.	斜体的
lenient	adj.	温和的，轻的
nonpayment	n.	不支付
omit	vt.	省略
overdue account		过期未付账款
overlook	vt.	忽视，未注意
over-trading		过分交易，经营过多
proceed with		进行
receipt	n.	收据
region	n.	地区
reminder letter		催收账款信函
remittance	n.	汇款

repayment	n.	偿还，归还款，偿还
run out of		消耗完，用完
session	n.	会议
signature	n.	签名
suit	n.	诉讼
Sydney	n.	悉尼
tangible asset		有形资产
tie up		占用
voucher	n.	发票，凭证
weak spot		弱点

 Notes

　　一般来说，买方付款及时，有时迟几天，在这种情况下无须催款。如果拖欠时间过长，就有必要向买方发出第一封催收信（collection of first reminder）。第一封催收信一般向买方寄去盖章的账单（statement of account）副本，目的是提醒客户，规定付款时间已过，有礼貌地提醒对方付款。如果第一封信件发出若干天（10天）仍未收到回音，可以发出第二封催收信（second communication）。这类信函有印刷好的统一格式。在等待较长一段时间后，如仍无回音，可再次发出催收信，此时，信中语气较为强硬。最后一封催收信实际上是给客户最后一个机会，要求在某个时间前付款，否则将依法处理。

6.4　The Profit and Loss Account
（损益账户）

　　In this passage you will look at another financial document: the profit and loss account. This compares what the company spent to make those sales. You can look at a company's financial performance over the past year and describe what has happened.

RTX		
Profit and Loss Account for the Year Ended		
31 December		
	This year	Last year
Turnover	£1460	£2200
Cost of sales	1100	900
Gross profit	360	1300

		(continued)
Expenses		
Overheads	500	700
Depreciation	90	80
Operating profit	(230)	520
Investments	80	120
Interest payable	(300)	(200)
Profit/(loss) on ordinary activities after tax	(450)	(440)
Dividends	25	60
Retained profit	(475)	(380)

6.5 Annual Report: Chairman's Statement
（年度报告）

Report

The purpose of this report is to tell you about RTX's performance over the past year and to outline our plans and prospects for next year. This year has not been a good one for RTX. There has been a dramatic fall in turnover as a result of a new competitor in the market. Our investments have also gone down because of poor financial investing. This has led to a decrease in both profit and dividends. Looking now towards the future, we hope that next year we will see an increase in turnover and profits again. We now have to face the challenge of having a serious new competitor so we are going to change our investment and we are going to move into new markets in Eastern Europe where prices are still low and there are many opportunities. To conclude, while this has been a bad year for RTX, the prospects for the next 12 months look good.

Chairman's Statement

I am pleased to report an excellent performance for the year ended 30 April. Turnover has increased by 130% to $1,153 million (last year—$501 million); profit before tax is up 176% to $120.5 million (last year—$43.6 million) and earnings per share have risen 102% to 39.7 pence (last year—19.7 pence).

A final dividend of 6.0 pence per share (last year—4.6 pence) is proposed and payable to those ordinary shareholders on the register on 15 August. The total dividend for the year is 9.0 pence, up 34% last year and covered four times by profit for the financial year.

The figures reflect our achievement in moving the group from being the UK bus market leader to a more broadly based transport business with significant international interests. The railway acquisitions of SWT and Porterbrook, together with the purchase of the largest bus and coach operator in Scandinavia, have positioned us strongly in exciting new markets.

The Stagecoach challenge in the UK bus market is to distinguish itself as an organic growth business. We have been able to increase passenger volumes for the fourth year running and the current year increase of 1.7% is against a background of continued sector decline.

Overseas, the acquisition of Swebus was completed in October. We believe that our strong market position in Sweden will increase our ability to capitalize on future growth opportunities in other European countries which deregulate bus services and follow the Swedish model of competitive tendering. Swebus Express relaunched its Stockholm-Gothenburg-Malmo service using our tried and tested inter-urban principles. The results have been outstanding with an increase in passenger traffic from 60,000 per month to 140,000 per month and we have placed an order for 75 coaches as there is enormous potential to expand the express market in Sweden.

In its first full year in the Stagecoach group, SWT have made good progress towards achieving its targets of increased revenue, better punctuality and reliability and the provision of more peak trains and seating capacity. This progress was hindered in February and March by train cancellations following implementation problems with SWT's driver restructuring initiative. The position was redressed from the beginning of April and SWT is now back on course to meet current and future targets.

Success at SWT will position the group for further rail opportunities and a key task will be to identify and develop experienced rail managers and staff capable of taking effective advantage of such opportunities.

Porterbrook has proved to be an excellent acquisition for Stagecoach. I am pleased to report that Porterbrook has secured, or been announced as preferred bidder for, £280 million of new train orders (including £90 million for SWT) in the last six months.

The global opportunities for Stagecoach over the year ahead remain exciting and I look forward to 12 months of further challenging developments. The current year has started well and the directors believe that the prospects for each of our businesses remain good. I am confident that our carefully targeted expansion programmes across all our businesses will result in strong growth in earnings for the future.

 New Words, Phrases and Special Terms

| acquisition | n. | 取得，获得 |
| background | n. | 背景 |

bidder	n.		投标人，投标商
cancellation	n.		取消
capitalize	vt.		发行股票，长期投资
predict	v.		预言，预测，预告
redress	vt.	n.	纠正
session	n.		会议，会期；开庭
share	n.		份额，股份，股票
vehicle	n.		运载工具，车辆，机动车
depreciation	n.		折旧
dividend	n.		股利
gross profit			总利润
hinder	v.		阻碍
implementation	n.		执行
negative	adj.		负的
operating profit			营业利润
overheads	n.		管理费用
profit and loss			损益
provision	n.		供应
relaunch	v.		重新发动
restructure	vt.		重组，调整改革
retained earnings			留存收益，未分配利润
tender	n.		招标，投标
turnover	n.		营业额

 Notes

1. The purpose of this report is to tell you about RTX's performance over the past year and to outline our plans and prospects for next year.

这篇年度报告要告诉你 RTX 在过去一年里的业绩，并简述明年的计划和设想。

2. Looking now towards the future, we hope that next year we will see an increase in turnover and profits again.

展望未来，我们希望在明年又能看到在营业额和利润方面有所增长。

3. To conclude, while this has been a bad year for RTX, the prospects for the next 12 months look good.

总而言之，RTX 公司过去一年很糟糕，但预期未来一年前景美好。

6.6 Setting up in Business
(创立企业)

Careful Preparation Increases Your Chances of Success

270,000 businesses started trading during the first six months of this year—a 10% increase on last year.

227,000 small businesses closed in the same period—a decrease of 15% on last year.

Research shows that the majority of people setting up their own businesses or becoming self-employed do it for the independence. How can these would be entrepreneurs, who work extremely long hours and put their family and security at risk, reduce the chances of failure?

In addition to the skills required to "do the job", do you have the discipline to work on your own, make decisions and turn your hand to everything from washing up coffee cups to doing the books? Can you handle the long hours coupled with the pressure? Do you have the support of your family?

Have you done your market research? Your family and friends may buy from you but that will not be enough. Remember that the product or service you are selling needs to be something that a customer wants not just today or next week. Ideally you need a number of customers buying once or a selection of customers buying regularly. Assuming that you are sure of what your customer wants, you need to know why it is that they will buy from you. Remember —without customers you will not have a business.

How will potential customers know you are there? You need to consider marketing and selling. This is when you will discover that there can be significant costs involved. How many customers do you need to reach? What percentage of them is likely to buy? How much is it costing you to reach each one? What are your sales forecasts?

What do you need to supply this level of sales:premises,stock,vehicles,time? The list can appear endless and always costs more than you thought. This in itself raises two further concerns: If these are your costs, were your calculations on pricing right? Will you make a profit? If you change your prices, will potential customers still buy at all or in the same volumes?

It will be at about this stage that you will realize the actual amount of money required to start the business. Have you got it? The financial requirements of the business need to be carefully planned. Identify how much you need to get the business started, how much you will need to keep the business going whilst sales build and cash starts to come in at a sufficiently high level from you customers.

What do you require to cover all your costs and, in the medium term, enough surplus to provide you with the minimum you personally need to survive after tax and national insurance have been met?

Simply stated, the above forms are the core of planning a new business. Business planning is essential to the successful development of the business. Correctly completed it can help you set the targets against which you can monitor yourself to ensure that you are keeping on track. It can also test the viability of your proposition and will indicate whether you have a potential new business on your hands or if you should rethink your idea.

If all this seems daunting, help and advice is available from Business Link. A team of experienced small business counselors provide a free, impartial and confidential counseling service which includes assistance in developing your ideas, information on legal requirements, how to do market research and prepare a business plan.

Discussing a Business Plan

Helen and Alex discuss Alex's business plan.

Helen　Hello, Alex. How are you getting on with your business plan?

Alex　Oh, fine. I'm going to speed this weekend working out the finances and I'll have finished it by Monday.

Helen　Have you remembered everything? Have you considered health and safety legislation, for example?

Alex　Oh no, I haven't. I'll find out about it.

Helen　What about your personal budget?

Alex　I think I'll need about £12,000 to cover my personal expenses for the first year.

Helen　That's not very much.

Alex　I know, but I've decided I'm not going to have a holiday this year. Anyway, this time next year I'll be earning millions.

Helen　So you're optimistic that you'll succeed then?

Alex　Of course, I expect to be succeed, I wouldn't start my own business if I wasn't optimistic.

Helen　Have you made an appointment with the bank manager yet?

Alex　Yes, I'm seeing her on Wednesday morning.

Helen　What does your girlfriend think of your plan?

Alex　Oh, she's too busy to care. She's about to start a new job.

Helen　Why don't we meet up on Tuesday and go over the plan together before you see the bank manager?

Alex　Yes, that'd be great. I'll give you a call.

A Business Plan Layout

A business plan usually follows the layout shown by the list of headings below:

1. Executive summary

This is a summary that gives the reader an idea of the plan, including information on the products or services, the management of the business, finance and anticipated sales.

2. Nature of the business

This section of the plan communicates the business idea, why you think it'll be successful, and the aims and objective of the business. It describes the type of business and type of company, and gives details of starting dates, etc.

3. Management of the business

This section of the plan gives details of the key people in the business and their relevant qualifications and experience. It also lists the skills and training needed in the future.

4. Sales and marketing

This very important section of the plan includes information that helps you decide, by reasonable judgment rather than intuition, whether there's a demand for the product or not and who your customers are. You should consider what makes you different from your competitors, your pricing and how to promote your business.

5. Product and services

This section describes what it is you're actually going to produce or offer and what you need in order to do so. You need to consider suppliers, quality, stocks and costs, reviewing and developing what you offer as demand changes.

6. Premises, equipment and vehicles

This section of the plan describes where you are going to set up your business and what you need in order to supply your product or service. You need to think about rent, lacation, legal implications, tax, costs, etc.

7. Legal and insurance

This section includes information about setting up partnerships or limited companies, property leases, licensing, patents, copyright, terms of employment, health and safety regulations, and covering yourself for when things go wrong.

8. Financial planning—profit and loss

This section includes start-up costs, a sales forecast showing what you expect to sell in the first year (not confusing sales with cash), and the cost of sales and your overheads (heating, lighting, advertising, etc.). It's a good idea to overestimate your costs and underestimate your sales.

9. Monitoring performance—cash-flow forecast

This section identifies when money comes into and goes out of the business over a period of time.

10. Personal survival budget

This section covers how much you will need to live on while setting up your business, taking into account tax, food, your home, family, clothes, personal pensions, etc.

11. Assessing profitability

In this section you should calculate your "breakeven point", i.e. how much you need to sell before you start to make a profit.

12. Contingency plans/risk assessment

This section outlines what you will do if circumstances change or something unexpected happens and things don't go according to plan.

New Words, Phrases and Special Terms

assessment	n.	估价，估定
breakeven point		盈亏平衡点
confidential	adj.	保密的
context	n. adj.	上下文的，上下文一致的
contingency	n.	偶然性
daunting	adj.	令人畏缩的
discipline	n.	训练，修养，纪律
entrepreneur	n.	企业家
essential	adj.	重要的，关键；基本的，主要的
establish	v.	设立；确立；
impartial	adj.	没有偏见的，不偏不倚的
intuition	n.	直觉
leaflet	n.	传单；活页
literature	n.	文学，文献，著作
loan	n.	借债，贷款
personality	n.	个性
phrase	n.	短语；习惯用语
potential	n. adj.	可能性；潜在力
premise	n.	（企业用）房屋等建筑物
profit	n.	利润，收益；益处
questionnaire	n.	问卷，调查卷

viability   n.   生存能力，生命力

 Section II   Review & Exercises（复习与练习）

 **Summary**

1. Match each of the following words and expressions with its definition.

   (1) dividend   (a) a payment to shareholders when a company has made a profit

   (2) invoice   (b) ordinary shares

   (3) liabilities   (c) The person who takes on the responsibility for checking a company's accounts

   (4) revenue   (d) when a company first sells its shares on the stock exchange

   (5) working capital   (e) possessions which can be converted into cash

   (6) assets   (f) goods which are not wanted after all, usually because they are faulty

   (7) float on the stock exchange   (g) a list of goods which have been sent to a customer indicating the amount charged to their account

   (8) returns   (h) someone to whom we owe money

   (9) equities   (i) debts which will have to be paid either now or in the future

   (10) auditor   (j) capital that is used to run a business on a day-to-day basis and is not invested in buildings, equipment

   (11) depreciation   (k) money received from sales

   (12) debtor   (l) people who owe us money

   (13) creditor   (m) the fall in the value of an asset as a result of usage or waste

2. Companies in many countries are required by law to report their financial situation to shareholders in an annual report. The annual report includes three main financial statements: the balance sheet, the profit and loss account and the cash-flow forecast. Look at the table below and match each document with its correct definition.

(1) The annual report	(a) This statement shows the revenue earned from sales (income) against all the costs related to those sales.
(2) The profit and loss account	(b) This statement shows where cash comes from and where it goes over a period of time.

(continued)

(3) The cash-flow forecast	(c) This document is produced once a year, reports back to shareholders what happened to the business over the year.
(4) The balance sheet	(d) This statement shows an organization's assets (what it owns) against its liabilities (what it owns) at a particular time—usually the beginning or end of a financial period, such as a month or a year.

Questions

1. A company's balance sheet lists the sources of a company's finance (its assets), and the money that a company owes (its liabilities). Which of the following items are assets and which are liabilities?

	Assets	Liability
(1) Loans to be repaid	☐	☐
(2) Buildings owned by the company	☐	☐
(3) Land owned by the company	☐	☐
(4) Taxes to be paid	☐	☐
(5) Money owned to suppliers	☐	☐
(6) Vehicles owned by the company	☐	☐
(7) Cash in the bank	☐	☐
(8) Money owned to the company	☐	☐
(9) Goods for sale	☐	☐

2. Assets can be divided into different types. Fixed assets are things which the company is expected to own for a long time. Current assets are things which the company can convert quickly into cash. Which of the assets identified in Problem 1 are fixed assets and which are current assets?

3. Look at the balance sheet for Marks and Spencer. Match the underlined words and expressions with the definitions below.

(1) What the company owns and is expected to own for a long time.

(2) What the company owns in short term that can quickly be converted into cash.

(3) Something owned by the company has a material form, such as machines, goods or cash.

(4) What the company owns in the short term, to be paid back within a year, such as money borrowed from the bank, money the company owns to suppliers, expenses it has incurred but not settled yet or money owned to tax authorities and shareholders.

(5) People who owe the company money.

(6) People the company owes money to.
(7) Supplies of resources or goods for sale, use or distribution (in a shop, warehouse, etc.).
(8) The financial worth of a company (assets minus liabilities).

Marks and Spencer Half-Year Results

Consolidated Profit and loss account

	26 weeks ended		
	27 Sept 2005 £m	28 Sept 2004 £m	Increase/ (decrease) %
Turnover			
Continuing operations	3,742.4	3,533.5	5.9
Operating profit			
Continuing operations	418.9	401.3	4.4
Loss on sale of property and other fixed assets	(1.2)	(1.4)	(14.3)
Net interest income	34.6	30.2	14.6
Profit on ordinary activities before taxation	452.3	430.1	5.2
Taxation on ordinary activities	(135.7)	(135.0)	0.5
Profit on ordinary activities after taxation	316.6	295.1	7.3
Minority interests (all equity)	0.3		
Profit attributable to shareholders	316.9	295.1	7.4
Dividends	(102.7)	(93.3)	10.1
Undistributed surplus for the period	214.2	201.8	6.2
Earning per share	11.14p	10.46p	6.5
Dividend per share	3.60p	3.30p	9.1

Consolidated balance sheet

	As at 27 Sept 2005 £m	As at 28 Sept 2004 £m
Fixed assets		
Tangible assets	4,007.3	3,480.6
Investments	83.8	48.8
	4,091.1	**3,529.4**
Current assets		
Stocks	492.7	437.2
Debtors	1,799.3	1,430.6
Cash and investments	892.2	1,117.0
	3,184.2	**2,984.8**
Current liabilities		
Creditors: amounts falling due within one year	1,843.5	1,531.9
Net current assets	**1,340.7**	**1,452.9**
Total assets less current liabilities	**5,431.8**	**4,982.3**
Creditors: amounts falling due after more than one year	581.1	578.1
Provisions for liabilities and charges	31.7	32.9
Net assets	4,819.0	4,371.3
Capital and reserves		

Called up share capital	713.0	706.8
Share premium account	289.3	244.8
Revaluation reserve	456.3	449.8
Profit and loss account	3,342.4	2,949.4
Shareholders' funds (all equity)	4,801.0	4,350.8
Minority interests (all equity)	18.0	20.5
Total capital employed	**4,819.0**	**4,371.3**

Solved Problems

1. In financial presentations you often use graphs, charts, diagrams and tables, but what's the difference between them? Read the text below, and label the examples.

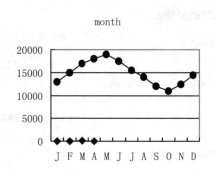

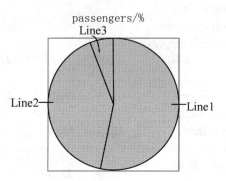

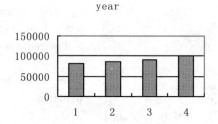

Line	Punctuality Record year D	Punctuality Target year E
1	94%	97%
2	92.5%	96%
3	85%	91%

Chapter 6 Review: Financial Awareness (复习：财务意识)

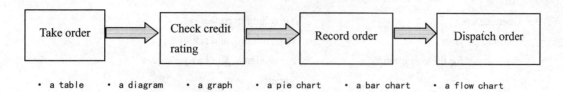

- a table
- a diagram
- a graph
- a pie chart
- a bar chart
- a flow chart

Antonio Zannetti, Director of A–Z Trains, gives a presentation about the company's performance and plans.

Good morning, ladies and gentlemen. My name's Antonio Zannett and I'm the Director of A–Z Trains.

Today I'm going to talk about passenger numbers on our three lines. First I'll tell you about Lines 1 and 2, where we've been successful over the past year, then I'll talk about Line 3, where our performance has been disappointing, and finally I'll outline our future for all three lines.

As you can see from Bar Chart, passenger numbers have increased steadily on Lines 1 and 2 as a result of our competitive policy on fares and our successful advertising campaign last autumn.

Now let's turn to Line 3, where we haven't been so successful and we found that our targets were overoptimistic. If you look at Line Graph you'll see that passenger numbers dropped dramatically in June as a result of industrial action by our drivers.

Turning to our plans for the next 12 months, we hope to increase passenger numbers on all three lines by continuing with our current fares policy and by offering loyalty cards to our regular customers.

So, to conclude, while the past year has generally been successful for A－Z Trains in terms of passenger numbers, we hope that over the next 12 months we'll be able to build on that success and eliminate the problems we've had. Thank you for your attention.

2. You now have your basic business plan ready, but you need to think about the finances. Calculate what the approximate start-up and overheads will be for the business you chose, for example, an ice-cream shop.

Start-up costs include	**Overheads include**
Equipment (telephone, fax, computer)	Rent
	Heating, lighting and phone bills
Vehicles and special equipment	Wages
Deposit and initial rent	Bank charges and interest
Telephone installation	Insurance
Insurance	

Opening stock   Travelling expenses
Stationery / printing   Post, printing and stationery
Staff wages for the first month   Accountants' and Lawyers' fees
                                       Repairs
                                       Advertising
                                       Depreciation (of vehicles and equipment)

Section III Reading Material (阅读材料)

Statement of Cash Flows

Usually a business must include the statement of cash flows in its financial reports as a complement to the income statement and balance sheet. The main purpose of the statement of cash flows is to report the cash inflows (or cash receipts) and the cash outflows (or cash disbursements) during an accounting period. The difference between the cash inflows and the cash outflows is referred to as a business's net cash flows.

The information of a business's cash flows is important to the financial statements' users. With the statement of cash flows, the financial statement users can get the information on the timing, amounts, and causes of the cash inflows and the cash outflows during all accounting period. They can evaluate business's liquidity and project its future cash flows. In addition, management may use the statement of cash flows to assess the debt-paying ability of the business, determine *dividend policy* (股利政策), and plan investing and financing needs, In accordance with the requirement of the generally accepted accounting standards, the statement of cash flows should explain the differences between the beginning balances and the ending balances of cash and *cash equivalents* (现金等价物). Cash equivalents are the short-term investments that must meet two following criteria: (1) the investment must be readily convertible to a known amount of cash; (2) the investment must be sufficiently close to its maturity date so that its market value is relatively insensitive to interest rate changes. Examples of cash equivalents include temporary investments in U.S. *treasury bill* (国库券), *commercial paper* (商业票据), and *money market funds* (货币市场基金). Exhibit shows the content of the statement of cash flows.

In the Exhibit 1, note that the cash flows are classified into three categories: cash flows from operating activities, cash flows from investing activities, and cash flows from financing activities.

Operating activities are day-to-day operations of a business. They include the purchasing and selling of goods for a merchandising company or the performing of services for a service company and the expenditures related to administering a business. Examples of cash inflows from operating activities are cash sales to customers, cash collections from credit customers, receipts of cash dividends from stock investment and receipts of interest payment. The primary cash outflows from operating activities include payments to supplies of goods and services, payments to employees for salaries and wages, interest payment and cash refund to customers.

Investing activities involve the buying and selling of stocks and bonds of other companies (other than the investments classified as cash equivalents), buying and selling non current assets such as plant assets, and making and collecting loans (notes receivables current or noncurrent other than the notes resulted from sales to customers).

Financing activities include the business's transactions with its owners and long-term creditors such as the buying and selling of the business's own stock (or investments for single proprietorships and partnerships), payments of dividends to its owners (or withdrawals for single proprietorships and partnerships), borrowing and repayments of loans (other than the notes resulted from the credit purchase of merchandise).

The information which is needed or the preparation of the statement of cash flows comes from an income statement for an accounting period, a comparative balance sheet（比较资产负债表）at the beginning and the end of the same period, and a careful analysis of each noncash balance sheet account. For the illustration purpose, Exhibit 2, Exhibit 3 and Exhibit 4 are presented to show the income statement, the comparative balance sheet, the statement of cash flows prepared by Great Prospect Company.

Exhibit 1

THE COMPANY NAME
Statement of Cash Flows
The Period of Time Covered

Cash flows from operating activities:

…

Net cash provided by operating activities

Cash flows from Investing Activities:

…

Net cash provided by investing activities

Cash flows from financing activities:

…

Net cash provided by financing activities

Net increase (decrease) in cash and cash equivalents

Cash and cash equivalents balance at beginning

Cash and cash equivalents balance at end

Exhibit 2

Great Prospect Company
Income Statement
For the Year Ended Dec. 31, 2005

Sales Revenues	$140,000
Less: Cost of Goods sold	−67,000
Gross Margin on sales（销售毛利）	$73,000
Operating Expenses	
Selling Expenses	
Sales Salaries	$9,000
Advertising and Promotion	8,000
Depreciation Expense	4,000
Insurance	2,000
Total Selling Expense	$23,000
General and Administrative Expenses	
Administrative Salaries	$8,000
Depreciation Expense	4,000
Insurance	2,000
Total General and Administrative Expenses	14,000
Total Operating Expenses	37,000
Pretax Income	$36,000
Income Tax on Normal Operations	9,000
Income before Extraordinary Item（非常项目）	27,000
Extraordinary Items	
Gain on Disposal of Long-term Investment (net of tax)	1,000
Net Income	$28,000
Earnings per Share （EPS，每股收益）of Common Stock	
Income before Extraordinary Items	$2.46
Extraordinary Items	0.09
Net Income	$2.55

Exhibit 3

Great Prospect Company
Comparative Balance Sheet

	Dec. 31, 2004	Dec. 31, 2005
Current Assets		
Cash	$40,000	$52,000
Accounts Receivable	20,000	17,000
Inventory	<u>30,000</u>	<u>35,000</u>
Total Current Assets	$90,000	$104,000
Long-term Investment		
Long-term Investment, shares of A Co.	<u>$10,000</u>	<u>$3,000</u>
Total Long-term Investment	10,000	3,000
Plant and Equipment		
Machinery and Equipment (net)	<u>$80,000</u>	<u>$75,000</u>
Total Plant and Equipment	80,000	75,000
Total Assets	<u>$180,000</u>	<u>$182,000</u>
Liabilities		
Current Liabilities		
Accounts Payable	$15,000	$11,000
Income Tax Payable	<u>4,000</u>	<u>6,000</u>
Total Current Liabilities	$19,000	$17,000
Long-term Liabilities		
Long-term Note Payable	$20,000	10,000
Bonds Payable	<u>30,000</u>	<u>10,000</u>
Total Long-term Liabilities	<u>50,000</u>	<u>20,000</u>
Total Liabilities	<u>$69,000</u>	<u>$37,000</u>
Shareholders' Equity		
Paid-in Capital		
Capital Stock, Common Stock, par $10, 10,000 shares issued and outstanding	$100,000	$110,000
Premium on Common stock	<u>8,000</u>	<u>11,000</u>
Total Paid-in Capital	$108,000	$121,000

Retained Earnings	3,000	24,000
Total Shareholders' Equity	$111,000	$145,000
Total Liabilities and Shareholders' Equity	$180,000	$182,000

Exhibit 4

Great Prospect Company
Statement of Cash Flows
For the Year Ended Dec.31, 2005

Cash flows from operating activities			
Cash received from customers	$143,000	(1)	
Cash payment for merchandise	(76,000)	(2)	
Payments for salaries and other operating expenses	(29,000)	(3)	
Payments for income tax	(7,000)	(4)	
Net Cash provided by Operating activities			$31,000
Cash flows from investing activities			
Cash received from disposal of machinery	$11,000		
Cash received from sale of long-term investment	7,000		
Cash paid for acquisition of equipment	(13,000)		
Net cash provided by investing activities			$5,000
Cash flows from financing activities（融资活动）			
Cash received from issuance of capital stock *	$13,000		
Cash paid for long-term note	(10,000)		
Cash paid for bonds	(20,000)		
Cash paid for cash dividends	(7,000)		
Net Cash provided by financing activities			(24,000)
Net increase in cash			$12,000
Cash balance at beginning of 2005			40,000
Cash balance at end of 2005			$52,000

Acquired equipment and paid in full by issuing 1,000 shares of common stock which had a market value of $ 13,000. The transaction is reported both as a *cash inflows*（现金流入）and *cash outflows*（现金流出）.

(1) Cash received from customers = Sales Revenues + Decrease in Accounts Receivable (or Increase in Accounts Receivable) = $140,000 + $ 3,000 = $143,000

(2) Cash payment for merchandise = Cost of goods sold + Increase in inventory (or − Decrease in Inventory) + Decrease in Accounts Payable (or − Increase in Accounts Payable)
$$= \$ 67,000 + \$5,000 + \$4,000$$
$$= \$ 76,000$$

(3) Payments for salaries and other operating expenses = Operating expenses other than depreciation + Increase in prepaid expense (or − Decrease in prepaid expense) + Decrease in accrued liabilities (or a Increase in accrued liabilities)
$$= \$ 37,000 - \$ 8,000$$
$$= \$ 29,000$$

(4) Payment for income taxes = Income taxes + Decrease in income tax payable (or − Increase in income tax payable) = $9,000 − $ 2,000
$$= \$7,000$$

Appendix 1

Accounting Law of the People's Republic of China

（中华人民共和国会计法）

(Originally Adopted at the Ninth Meeting of the Standing Committee of the Sixth of National People's Congress on January 21, 1985, as Amended at the Fifth Session of the Standing Committee of the Eighth National People's Congress on December 29, 1993)

Chapter I General Provisions

Article 1. This law is formulated in order to standardize and improve accounting work, ensure that accountants will function in accordance with law, and bring into play the role of accounting in safeguarding the order of the socialist market economy, strengthening economic administration and improving economic efficiency.

Article 2. State bodies, public organizations, enterprises, institutions, self-employed Industrialists and businessmen and other organizations shall execute their accounting matters in accordance with this law.

Article 3. The accountancy body and personnel must observe the laws and decrees set down in this Law and abide by them when carrying on the business of accounting and performing accountancy supervision.

Article 4. The leader of a unit shall supervise the accountant departments, account-ants and other personnel in implementing this law; make sure that accounting data are lawful, truthful, accurate and complete; and ensure that the functions and powers of accountants are not infringed upon. No one is allowed to retaliate against an accountant.

Accountants who carry out this Law conscientiously, devote themselves to their duties and achieve remarkable success in their work will be rewarded appropriately.

Article 5. The financial department of the State Council shall administer the work of national accountancy.

The financial department of the local people's government at various levels shall administer accountancy in their region.

Article 6. The national unified accounting system is formulated by the financial department of the State Council in line with this Law.

Financial departments of the provinces, autonomous regions and municipalities, competent departments of the State Council and the General Logistics Department of the People's Liberation Army may, under the precondition of not contravening this law and uniform state accounting systems, formulate specific procedures or supplementary provisions for implementing uniform state accounting systems and submit them to the financial authorities for approval or for the record.

Chapter II Business Accounting

Article 7. The following matters should go through accounting procedures and business accounting:

(1) Receipts and payments of funds and/or securities;

(2) The receipt and disposal, increase and decrease and use of a piece of property;

(3) Occurrence and settlement of a credit or debt;

(4) Increase or reduction of capital and funds as well as income and outlays;

(5) Calculations of revenue, expenses or costs;

(6) Calculation and treatment of financial achievements; and

(7) Any other matters necessary for going through accounting procedures and business accounting.

Article 8. The financial year begins on 1 January and ends on 31 December of the Gregorian calendar.

Article 9. Renminbi shall be the unit used in accounting books.

Units whose primary income and outlays are in foreign currency (currencies) may choose a certain foreign currency as the unit used for accounting purposes. In such cases, the currency shall be converted into renminbi when compiling accounting statements.

Article 10. Accounting proofs, accounting books, accounting statements and other accounting data shall conform to provisions regarding uniform state accounting systems.

Forgery or alteration of accounting proofs or accounting books or submission of false accounting statements are not allowed.

When computers are used in accounting, requirements regarding software used and the accounting proofs, accounting books, accounting statements and other accounting data generated therefrom shall conform to State Council and Ministry of Finance provisions.

Article 11. In handling the matters listed in Article 7 of this Law, original vouchers must be filed or presented, and should be handed over to the accounting body in good time. The accounting body must examine the original vouchers and draw up accounting vouchers on the basis of the examined original vouchers.

Article 12. Units may set up their own accounting departments and accounts books in accordance with the provisions of the accounting system.

The accounting body, according to the examined original vouchers and accounting vouchers, shall calculate accounts in line with the provisions of the accounting system.

Article 13. Units should set up a property-checking system to ensure that the accounting records conform with the quantities of existing materials and funds.

Article 14. Units shall compile accounting statements according to the uniform state accounting systems and on the basis of accounting books and submit them to the Ministry of Finance and other departments concerned.

Accounting reports should be signed or sealed by the unit's administrative head, the leading member of the accounting body and the accountant in charge. Units with a general accountant should also have their accounting reports signed or sealed by him or her.

Article 15. Vouchers, accounts books, reports and other accounting data should be filed and well kept in accordance with the related rules of the State. The time limits for the keeping of accounting files and the methods of their destruction will be decided by the financial department of the State Council jointly with the departments concerned.

Chapter III Accounting Supervision

Article 16. The accounting body and accounting personnel in various units may practise accounting supervision in their own units.

Article 17. The accounting body and accounting personnel should not accept or handle any false or illegal vouchers and should return any inaccurate and incomplete vouchers for correction or completion.

Article 18. When the accounting body and accounting personnel find that differences exist between accounting records and quantities of existing materials and funds, they should deal with them according to the relevant provisions; if the required authority is not held by the particular accounting body or personnel it should immediately be reported to the administrative head of their unit, in order that the truth may be discovered and a decision made.

Article 19. Accounting agencies or accountants shall refuse to handle illegal income and outlays.

Accounting agencies or accountants shall take action to stop or correct illegal income and outlays; where their action is ineffectual, they shall submit a written memorandum asking the unit's leader to handle it. The unit's leader shall, within ten days of receipt of the memorandum, make a decision which shall be put in writing, to which he is held accountable.

Accounting agencies or accountants who neither take action to stop or correct illegal income and outlays nor submit a written memorandum to the unit's leader are also held accountable.

Accounting agencies or accountants shall report to the competent unit or financial, auditing, taxation authorities about income and outlays that are severely harmful to the state and public interest. Authorities receiving such a report have the responsibility to deal with it.

Article 20. Various units must, in accordance with the law and related stipulations of the state, accept supervision of financial, auditing and taxation organizations and truthfully provide accounting vouchers, accounting books, accounting statements, ac-counting data and other related information. They must not reject such supervision or demand related documents and must not hide documents or make false reports.

Chapter IV   Accounting Bodies and Accounting Personnel

Article 21. Various units should establish accounting departments according to the accounting need or establish positions for accountants and designate a chief accountant in related departments. Units which do not have conditions for establishing accounting departments or hiring accountants may entrust approved accounting consultation and service organizations to do accounting work for them. Large and medium-sized enterprises and large business undertakings may set up a chief accountant, who must have qualifications as a professional accountant.

An accounts-checking system may be set up within an accounting body.

Cashiers may not concurrently hold responsibility for checking accounts, keeping accountting files and casting accounts of revenue, expenditure, credits or debits.

Article 22. The main duties of the accounting body and accounting personnel are:

(1) To make business accounting conform with the provisions of Chapter II of this Law;

(2) To practice accounting supervision in line with the provisions of Chapter III of this Law;

(3) To work out the main methods of handling accountancy matters within the unit itself;

(4) To take part in the drawing up of economic plans and business plans, and the checking and analysing of the implementation budget and financial plan; and

(5) To handle any other accounting business.

Article 23. Accounting personnel must have necessary professional knowledge. The appointment and removal of chief accountants or responsible persons of accounting departments of state-owned enterprises and business ventures must have the concurrence of higher units having jurisdiction over them. Chief accountants or responsible persons of accounting departments must not be appointed or removed willfully. If faithful accounting personnel who adhere to principles are treated in an improper manner, the higher units having jurisdiction over those enterprises or ventures should order those enterprises or ventures to take remedial measures. If accounting personnel neglect their duties, lack principles or are unsuitable for accounting work, the higher units should order concerned units to transfer or dismiss those unqualified accounting personnel.

Article 24. In the case of an accountant being removed or leaving his post, whether temporarily or permanently, he should conduct the handing over procedures in a competent manner with his successor.

Handing over procedures conducted by a common accountant should be supervised by a leading member of the accounting body or the accountant in charge. The procedures conducted by a leading member of the accounting body or the accountant in charge should be supervised by the administrative head of the unit and, if necessary, under the joint supervision of the administrative head of the unit and the person being replaced by the higher competent authority.

Chapter V   Legal Responsibility

Article 25. If any administrative head of a unit or any accounting personnel violate the provisions of business accounting set forth in Chapter II of this Law, they may have imposed on them administrative sanctions, if the case is of a serious nature.

Article 26. Leaders, accounting personnel and other staff members of various units who prepare false accounting vouchers, change or intentionally destroy vouchers, accounting books, accounting statements, accounting data and other related information, or if they use false accounting vouchers, accounting books, accounting statements and other accounting information and thus infringe upon interests of the state, society and the public shall be handled and investigated for their roles in these activities by financial, auditing, taxation and other related responsible units in accordance with the Law and administrative rules and regulations. Those whose actions constitute crimes shall be investigated for their criminal responsibility.

Article 27. Accounting personnel who accept and handle unlawful accounting vouchers, who do not make written comments to leaders of respective units on illegal income and expenditures, or if they do not make reports to higher units or financial, auditing and taxation organizations, will be given administrative punishment if the situation is serious. Accounting personnel who are responsible for major losses to government or private properties and whose actions constitute crimes shall be investigated for their criminal responsibility in accordance with the Law.

Article 28. If the leaders of various units, after receiving the written comments of accounting personnel in compliance with paragraph 2 of Article 19 of this law, still approve of such illegal income or expenditures or if they take no remedial action within a certain period without a proper reason and in this manner cause serious consequences,they shall be given administrative punishment. If their action or inaction causes severe harm to state and public interests and constitute crimes, they shall be investigated for their criminal responsibility.

Article 29. If an administrative head in a unit or other persons dispute the decisions of accountants who have carried out their duties in accordance with this Law, they should be imposed upon with administrative sanctions or investigated with regard to criminal responsibility in accordance with the Law, if the case is a serious one.

Chapter VI Supplementary Provisions

Article 30. This Law shall come into effect on May 1, 1985. Amendments to this Law shall come into force on the date of promulgation [December 29, 1993-1.]

Accounting Standard for Business Enterprises: Basic Standard

（企业会计准则——基本准则）

Chapter I General Provisions

Article 1. In accordance with "The Accounting Law of the People's Republic of China", this Standard is formulated to meet the needs of developing a socialist market economy in our country, to standardize accounting practice and to ensure the quality of accounting information.

Article 2. This Standard is applicable to all enterprises established within the territory of the People's Republic of China. Chinese enterprises established outside the territory of the People's Republic of China (hereinafter referred to as "enterprises abroad") are required to prepare and disclose their financial reports to appropriate domestic regulatory authorities in accordance with this Standard.

Article 3. Accounting systems of enterprises are required to comply with this Standard.

Article 4. An enterprise shall accurately account for all its transactions actually taken place in order to provide reports of reliable quality on the economic and financial activities of the enterprise itself.

Article 5. Accounting and financial reports should proceed on the basis that the enterprise is a continuing entity and will remain in operation into the foreseeable future.

Article 6. An enterprise shall account for its transactions and prepare its financial statements in distinct accounting periods. Accounting periods may be a fiscal year, a quarter, or a month, commencing on first days thereof according to the Gregorian calendar.

Article 7. The Renminbi is the bookkeeping base currency of an enterprise. A Foreign currency may be used as the bookkeeping base currency for enterprises which conduct transactions mainly in foreign currency. However, in preparing financial statements, foreign currency transactions are to be converted into Renminbi. This latter requirement applies to enterprises abroad when reporting financial and economic results to concerned domestic organizations.

Article 8. The debit and credit double entry bookkeeping technique is to be used for recording all accounting transactions.

Article 9. Accounting records and financial reports are to be compiled using the Chinese language. Minority or foreign languages may be used concurrently with the Chinese language by enterprises in autonomous areas of minority nationalities, or by enterprises with foreign investment, and by foreign enterprises.

Chapter II   General Principles

Article 10. The accounting records and financial reports must be based on financial and economic transactions as they actually take place, in order to objectively reflect the financial position and operating results of an enterprise.

Article 11. Accounting information must be designed to meet the requirements of national macro-economy control, the needs of all concerned external users to understand an enterprisers financial position and operating results, and the needs of management of enterprises to strengthen their financial management and administration.

Article 12. Accounting records and financial statements shall be prepared according to stipulated accounting methods, and accounting information of enterprises must be comparable and convenient to be analyzed.

Article 13. Accounting methods used shall be consistent from one period to the other and shall not be arbitrarily changed. Changes and reasons for changes, if necessary, and their impact on an enterprise's financial position and operating results, shall be reported in notes to the financial statements.

Article 14. Accounting and financial reports preparation must be conducted in a timely manner.

Article 15. Accounting records and financial reports shall be prepared in a clear, concise manner to facilitate understanding, examination and use.

Article 16. The accrual basis of accounting is to be adopted.

Article 17. Revenue shall be matched with related costs and expenses in accounting.

Article 18. Principle of prudence should be followed in reasonably determining the possible loss and expense.

Article 19. The values of all assets are to be recorded at historical costs at the time of acquisition. The amount recorded in books of account shall not be adjusted even though a fluctuation in their value may occur, except when State laws or regulations require specific treatment or adjustments.

Article 20. A clear distinction shall be drawn between revenue expenditures and capital expenditures. Expenditure shall be regarded as revenue expenditure where the benefit to the enterprise is only related to the current fiscal year; and as capital expenditure where the benefits to the enterprise last for several fiscal years.

Article 21. Financial reports must reflect comprehensively the financial position and operating results of an enterprise. Transactions relating to major economic activities are to be identified, appropriately classified, and accounted for, and separately reported in financial statements.

Chapter III Assets

Article 22. Assets are economic resources, which are measurable by money value, and which are owned or controlled by an enterprise, including all property, rights as a creditor to others, and other rights.

Article 23. For accounting treatment, assets are normally divided into current assets, long-term investments, fixed assets, intangible assets, deferred assets and other assets.

Article 24. Current assets refer to those assets which will be realized or consumed within one year of their acquisition, or within an operating cycle longer than a year. They include cash, cash deposits, short-term investments, accounts receivable, prepayments, and inventories, etc..

Article 25. Cash and all kinds of deposits shall be accounted for according to the actual amount of receipt and payment.

Article 26. Short-term investments refer to various of marketable securities, which can be realized at any time and will be held less than a year, as well as other investment with a life of no longer than a year.

Marketable securities shall be accounted for according to historical cost as obtained.

Income received or receivable from marketable securities in current period and the difference between the receipt obtained from securities sold and book cost shall be all accounted for as current profit or loss.

Marketable securities shall be shown in book balance in accounting statement.

Article 27. Receivables and prepayments include: notes receivable, accounts receivable, other receivables, accounts prepaid and prepaid expenses, etc..

Receivables and prepayments shall be accounted for according to actual amount.

Provision for bad debts may be set up on accounts receivable. The provision for bad debts shall be shown as a deduction item of accounts receivable in the financial statement.

All receivables and prepayments shall be cleared and collected on time, and shall be checked with related parties periodically. Any accounts receivable, proved to be definitely uncollectible according to state regulations, shall be recognized as bad debts and written off against provision for bad debts or charged to current profit or loss, if such provision is not set up.

Prepaid expenses shall be amortized according to period benefiting, and the balance shall be shown separately in accounting statement.

Article 28. Inventories refer to merchandise, finished goods, semifinished goods, goods in process, and all kinds of materials, fuels, containers, low-value and perishable articles and so on that stocked for the purpose of sale, production or consumption during the production operational process.

All inventories shall be accounted for at historical cost as obtained. Those enterprises keeping books at planned cost or norm cost in daily accounting shall account for the cost variances and adjust planned cost (or norm cost) into historical cost periodically.

When inventories issuing, enterprises may account them under the following methods: first-in first-out, weighted average, moving average, specific identification, last-in first-out, etc.

All inventories shall be taken stock periodically. If any overage, shortage and out-of-date, deterioration and damage that need to be scrapped shall be disposed within they ear and accounted into current profit or loss. All the inventories shall be disclosed at historical cost in accounting statement.

Article 29. Long-term investment refers to the investment impossible or not intended to be realized within a year, including shares investment, bonds investment and other investments.

In accordance with different situation, shares investment and other investments shall be accounted for by cost method or equity method respectively.

Bonds investment shall be accounted for according to actual amount paid. The interest accrued contained in the actually paid amount shall be accounted for separately.

Where bonds are acquired at a premium or discount, the difference between the cost and the face value of the bonds shall be amortized over the periods to maturity of the bonds.

Interest accrued during the period of bonds investment and the difference between the amount of principal and interest received on bonds sold and their book cost and interest accrued but not yet received shall be accounted for as current profit and loss.

Shares investment, bonds investment and other investments shall be shown separately in accounting statements at book balance.

Bonds investment matured within a year shall be shown in the accounting statements separately under the caption of current assets.

Article 30. Fixed assets refer to the assets whose useful life is over one year, unit value is above the prescribed criteria and where original physical form remains during the process of utilization, including building and structures, machinery and equipment, transportation equipment, tools and implement, etc..

Fixed assets shall be accounted for at historical cost as obtained. Interest of loan and other related expenses for acquiring fixed assets, and the exchange difference from conversion of foreign currency loan, if incurred before the assets not having been put into operation or after been put into operation but before the final account for completed project is made, shall be accounted as fixed assets value; if incurred after that, shall be accounted for as current profit or loss.

Fixed assets coming from donations shall be accounted through evaluation with reference to market price, wear and tear degree or determined the value with relevant evidence provided by contributors. Expenses incurred on receiving those donated fixed assets, shall be accounted for as the fixed assets value.

Fixed assets financed by leasing shall be accounted with reference of the way fixed assets are accounted and shall be explained in notes to the accounting statements.

Depreciation on the fixed assets shall be accounted according to state regulations. On the basis of the original cost, estimated residual value, the useful life of the fixed assets or estimated working capacity, depreciation on the fixed assets shall be accounted for on the straight line method or the working capacity (or output) method. If approved or conforming to relevant regulations, accelerated depreciation method may be adopted.

Fixed assets, original value, accumulated depreciation and its net value shall be shown separately in accounting statement.

The actual expenditures incurred in the purpose of acquiring or technical reforming the fixed assets before available to the users, shall be shown separately as construction in progress in accounting statement.

The fixed assets must be taken inventory periodically. The net profit or loss incurred in discard and disposal, and also overage, shortage of fixed assets shall be accounted as current profit and loss.

Article 31. Intangible assets refer to assets that will be used by an enterprise for along term without material state, including patents, nonpatented technology, trademark, copyrights, right to use sites, and goodwill, etc..

Intangible assets obtained through purchase shall be accounted for at actual cost. Intangible assets received from investors shall be accounted for at the assessed value recognised or the amount specified in the contract. Self-developed intangible assets shall be accounted at actual cost in the development process.

All intangible assets shall be averagely amortized periodically over the period benefitted from such expenditures and be shown with unamortized balance in accounting statement.

Article 32. Deferred assets refer to all the expenses that could not be accounted as current profit or loss totally but should be periodically amortized in future years, including organization expenses, expenditures incurred in major repair and improvement of the rented in fixed assets etc..

The expenses incurred in an enterprise during its preparation period shall be accounted for as organization expenses except those accounted into related property or material value. The organization expense shall be averagely amortized in a certain period of years after the operation starts.

Expenditures incurred on major repair and improvement of the rented in fixed assets shall be averagely amortized by years in the period of leasing.

All deferred assets shall be shown separately in accounting statements by its balance not yet amortized.

Article 33. Other assets refer to the long-term assets except all items mentioned above.

Chapter IV Liabilities

Article 34. A liability is debt borne by an enterprise, measurable by money value, which will be paid to a creditor using assets, or services.

Article 35. Liabilities are generally classified into current liabilities and long-term liabilities.

Article 36. Current liabilities refer to the debts which should be paid off within a year or an operating cycle longer than a year, including short-term loans payable, notes payable, accounts payable, advances from customers, accrued payroll, taxes payable, profits payable, dividends payable, other payables, provision for expenses, etc..

All current liabilities shall be accounted for at actual amount incurred. Liabilities incurred but the amount needed to be estimated shall be accounted for at a reasonable estimate, and then adjusted after actual amount was given.

Balance of current liabilities shall be shown by items in accounting statements.

Article 37. Long-term liabilities refer to the debts which will be redeemed after a year or an operating cycle longer than a year, including long-term loans payable, bonds payable, long-term accounts payable, etc..

Long-term loans payable include the loans borrowed from financial institutions and other units. It shall be accounted independently according to the different characters of the loan and at the amount actually incurred.

Bonds shall be accounted for at par value. When bonds are issued in premium or discount, the difference between the amount actually obtained and the par value shall be accounted independently, and be written off periodically by increasing or decreasing interest expenses of every period until bonds mature.

Long-term accounts payable include accounts payable for importing equipments, accounts payable for fixed assets financed by leasing. Long-term accounts payable shall be accounted at actual amounts.

Long-term liabilities shall be shown by items of long-term loans, bonds payable, long-term accounts payable in accounting statements.

Long-term liabilities to be matured and payable within a year shall be shown as a separate item under the caption of current liabilities.

Chapter V Owners' Equity

Article 38. Owners' equity refers to the interest of the investors remaining in the net assets of an enterprise, including capital of the enterprise invested in by investors, capital reserve, surplus reserve, and undistributed profit retained in the enterprise etc..

Article 39. Invested Capital is the capital funds actually invested in the enterprise by its investors, whether it is in form of cash, physical goods or other assets for the operation of the enterprise.

Invested Capital shall be accounted for at the amount actually invested.

Amount of shares issued by a corporation shall be accounted for as capital stock at the face value of the shares issued.

Special appropriation allocated by the government to an enterprise shall be accounted for as government investment unless otherwise provided.

Article 40. Capital reserve includes premium on capital stock, legal increment of property value through revaluation and value of donated assets accepted, etc..

Article 41. Surplus reserve refers to the reserve funds set up from profit according to relevant government regulations.

Surplus reserve shall be accounted for at the amount actually set up.

Article 42. Undistributed profit refers to the profit reserved for future distribution or not distributed yet.

Article 43. Invested capital, capital reserve, surplus reserve and undistributed profit shall be shown by items in accounting statement. Deficit not yet made up, if any, shall be shown as a deduction item of owners' equity.

Chapter VI Revenue

Article 44. Revenue refers to the financial inflows to an enterprise as a result of the sale of goods and services, and other business activities of the enterprise, including basic operating revenue and other operating revenue.

Article 45. Enterprises shall rationally recognize revenue and account for the revenue on time.

Enterprises generally recognize revenue when merchandise shipped, service provided as well as money collected or rights collecting money obtained.

Revenue of long-term project contract (including labor service) shall be reasonably recognized, in general, according to the completed progress method or the completed contract method.

Article 46. Return of sales, sales allowances and sales discount shall be accounted for as deduction items of operating revenue.

Chapter VII Expenses

Article 47. Expenses refer to the outlays incurred by an enterprise in the course of production and operation.

Article 48. Expenses directly incurred by an enterprise in production and service provision, including direct labor, direct materials, purchase price of commodities and other direct expenses shall be charged directly into the cost of production or operation;indirect expenses incurred in production and provision of service by an enterprise is to be allocated into the cost of production and operation, according to certain criteria of allocation.

Article 49. General and administrative expenses incurred by enterprise's administrative sectors for organizing and managing production and operation, financial expenses, purchase expenses on commodities purchased for sale, and sales expenses for selling commodities and providing service, shall be directly accounted for as periodic expense in the current profit and loss.

Article 50. The expenses paid in current period but attributable to the current and future periods shall be distributed and accounted for in current and future periods. The expenses attributable to the current period but not yet paid in current period shall be recognized as accrued expenses and charged to cost of the current period.

Article 51. Enterprises shall generally calculate products cost every month.

Costing methods shall be decided by the enterprise itself according to the characteristics of its production and operation, type of production management and requirements of cost management. Once it is decided, no change can be made arbitrarily.

Article 52. Enterprises shall calculate expenses and costs on actual amounts incurred. Those adopting the norm costing, or planned costing in accounting for daily calculation shall reasonably calculate the cost variances, and adjust them into historical cost at the end of the month while preparing accounting statements.

Article 53. Enterprises shall convert the cost of commodities sold and service pro-vided into operating cost accurately and timely, then account current profit and loss together with periodic expenses.

Chapter VIII   Profit and Loss

Article 54. Profit is the operating results of an enterprise in an accounting period, including operating profit, net investment profit and net non-operating income.

Operating profit is the balance of operating revenue after deducting operating cost, periodic expenses and all turnover taxes, surtax and fees.

Net investment profit is the balance of income on external investment after deducting investment loss.

Net non-operating income is the balance of non-operating income after deducting non-operating expenses. Non-operating income and expenses have no direct relating with the production operations of an enterprise.

Article 55. Loss incurred by an enterprise shall be made up according to the stipulated procedure.

Article 56. Items that constitute the profits and the distribution of profits shall be shown separately in the financial statement. A distribution of profit plan which is not yet approved at time of publication of a financial statement is to be identified in notes to the financial statement.

Chapter IX Financial Reports

Article 57. Financial reports are the written documents summarizing and reflecting the financial position and operating results of an enterprise, including a balance sheet, an income statement, a statement of changes in financial position (or a cash flow statement) together with supporting schedules, notes to the financial statements, and explanatory statements on financial condition.

Article 58. A balance sheet is an accounting statement that reflects the financial position of an enterprise at a specific date.

Items of the balance sheet should be grouped according to the categories of assets, liabilities and owners, equity, and shall be shown item by item.

Article 59. An income statement is an accounting statement that reflects the operating results of an enterprise within an accounting period, as well as their distribution.

Items of the income statement should be arranged according to the formation and distribution of profit, and shall be shown item by item.

Items of profit distribution part of the income statement may be shown separately in a statement of profit distribution.

Article 60. A statement of changes in financial position is an accounting statement that reflects comprehensively the sources and application of working capital and its changes during an accounting period.

Items of the statement of changes in financial position are divided into two groups: sources of working capital and application of working capital. The difference between the total sources and total applications is the net increase (or decrease) of the working capital. Sources of working capital are subdivided into profit sources and other sources; applications of working capital are also subdivided into profit distribution and other applications, all shall be shown item by item.

An enterprise may also prepare a cash flow statement to reflect the changes in its financial position.

A cash flow statement is an accounting statement that reflects the condition of cash receipts and cash disbursements of an enterprise during a certain accounting period.

Article 61. Financial statements should include comparative financial information for the corresponding previous accounting period. When so required, if the classification and contents of statement items of the previous accounting period are different from that of the current period, such items should be adjusted in conformity with that of the current period.

Article 62. Accounting statements should be prepared from the records of account books, completely recorded and correctly checked and other relative information. It is required that they must be true and correct in figures, complete in contents and issued on time.

Article 63. Consolidated financial statements shall be prepared by the enterprise(acts as a parent company) which owns 50% or more of the total capital of the enterprise it invested (acts as subsidiary) or otherwise owns the right of control over the invested enterprise. Financial statements of an invested enterprise of special line of business not suitable for consolidation, may not be consolidated, but should be submitted together with the consolidated financial statements of the parent company.

Article 64. Notes to the financial statements are explanatory to related items in the financial statement of the enterprise concerned so as to meet the needs to understand the contents of the statements. This should include mainly:

(1) the accounting methods adopted for the current and previous accounting periods;

(2) changes in accounting treatments between the current and prior periods, including the reasons for, and impact on the financial performance and status of the enterprise of such changes;

(3) description of unusual items;

(4) detailed information relating to major items listed in the accounting statements; and

(5) any other explanations necessary to provide users with a clear view and understanding of the financial statements.

Chapter X Supplementary Provisions

Article 65. The explanation of this Standard is the charge of the Ministry of Finance.

Article 66. This Standard will be effective as from 1 July, 1993.

Appendix 2

Glossary

（专业词汇总表）

account　　　n.　　　　　　　　账户，账目
A record of the increases and decreases of transactions summarized in an accounting form.

account numbers　　　　　　　账户编号
Numbers assigned to accounts according to the chart of accounts.

accountant　　n.　　　　　　　会计员，会计师
An individual who classifies and summarizes business transactions and interprets their effects on the business.

accounting　　n.　　　　　　　会计（学）
The process of analyzing, classifying, recording, summarizing, and interpreting business transactions.

accounts Payable　　　　　　　应付类账户
A liability account used by the business to keep a record of amounts due to creditors.

Accounts receivable　　　　　　应收类账户
Amount that is to be collected from customers.

accrual basis　　　　　　　　　权责发生制
An accounting system in which revenue is recognized only when earned, and expense is recognized only when incurred.

additional paid-in capital　　　　资本增值
Amounts paid in beyond the par value of stock.

adjusting entries　　　　　　　调整记录（分录）
Journal entries made at the end of an accounting period in order that the accounts will reflect the correct balance in the financial statements.

articles of copartnership　　　　（合伙企业中的）合伙协议

The written agreement among the partners that contains provisions on the formation, capital contribution, profit and loss distribution, admission, and withdrawal of partners.

  articles of incorporation　　　　　　（营业）执照，许可证

A charter submitted to the state by individuals wishing to form a corporation and containing significant information about the proposed business.

  assets　　　　　　n.　　　　　　资产

Properties owned that have monetary value.

  authorized shares　　　　　　被授权的，可发行的股份

Shares of stock that a corporation is permitted to issue (sell) under its articles of incorporation.

  average　　　　　　n.　　　　　　平均

A means of presenting large quantities of numbers in summary form.

  balance sheet　　　　　　资产负债表

A statement that shows the assets, liabilities, and capital of a business entity at a specific date. Also known as the statement of financial position.

  bank reconciliation　　　　　　银行调账单

A statement that reconciles the difference between the bank's balance and the balance of a company's books.

  bank service charge　　　　　　银行服务费，佣金，利息

A monthly charge made by the bank for keeping a depositor's checking account in operation.

  bank statement　　　　　　银行对账单

A periodic statement sent by the bank to its customers that presents the current balances of the cash account and provides a detailed list of all the payments made and all receipts received for a certain period of time.

  blank endorsement　　　　　　空白票据背书

Consists of only the name of the endorser on the back of the check.

  bonds　　　　　　n.　　　　　　基金

A form of long-term debt in which the corporation agrees to pay interest periodically and to repay the principal at a stated future date.

  book value per share　　　　　　每股账面价值

The amount that would be distributed to each share of stock if a corporation were to be dissolved.

  bookkeeper　　　　　　记账员，簿记员

An individual who earns a living by recording the financial activities of a business and who is concerned with the techniques involving the recording of transactions.

  cancelled checks　　　　　　已兑支票

Checks that have been paid by the bank during the month and returned to the depositor.

Appendix 2　Glossary（专业词汇总表）

Capital　n.　资本，业主权益，所有者权益
What an individual or business is worth. Also known as owners' equity.

capital Stock　股权（账户）
The account that shows the par value of the stock issued by the corporation.

cash disbursements journal　现金支出日记账
A special journal used to record transactions involving cash payments.

cash receipts journal　现金收入日记账
A special journal used to record transactions involving cash receipts.

certified check　（经银行授权）可兑现的支票
A check whose payment has been guaranteed by the bank.

chart of accounts　会计科目（账户名称）表
A listing of the accounts by title and numerical designation.

check　n.　支票
A written document directing the firm's bank to pay a specific amount of money to an individual.

checking account　支票账户
An account with a bank that allows the depositor to make payments to others from his or her bank balance.

closing entry　结账记录（分录）
An entry made at the end of a fiscal period in order to make the balance of a temporary account equal to zero.

closing the ledger　结转分类账
A process of transferring balances of income and expense accounts through the summary account to the capital account.

combined cash journal　（合并性）现金日记账
The journal with which all cash transactions are recorded.

common stock　普通股
That part of the capital stock that does not have special preferences or rights.

computer　计算机，电脑
A group of interconnected electronic machines capable of processing data.

computer hardware　计算机硬件
A term that refers to the actual physical components that make up an installation.

computer programs　计算机程序
A set of instructions developed by a programmer that tells the computer what to do, how to do it, and in what sequence it should be done.

computer software　计算机软件

The collection of programs and supplementary materials used by personnel to give the computer its instructions.

  controlling account   控制性账户

The account in the general ledger that summarizes the balances of a subsidiary ledger.

  conversion privilege   转换权（优先股转为普通股）

Given stockholders the option to convert preferred stock into common stock.

  corporation   公司

A business organized by law and viewed as an entity separate from its owners and creditors.

  cost of goods sold   商品销售成本

Inventory at the beginning of a fiscal period plus net purchases, less inventory at the end of the fiscal period. Also known as cost of sales.

  credit   n.   会计贷项，记入会计贷方

An amount entered on the right side of an account. Abbreviation is Cr.

  credit memorandum   买卖通知书

A receipt indicating the seller's acceptance to reduce the amount of a buyer's debt.

  current assets   流动资产

Assets that are expected to be realized in cash, sold, or consumed during the normal fiscal cycle of a business.

  current liabilities   流动负债

Debts that are due within a short period of time, usually consisting of 1 year, and which are normally paid from current assets.

  debit   n.   会计借项，记入会计借方

An amount entered on the left side of an account. Abbreviation is Dr.

  deposit in transit   在途存款

Cash deposited and recorded by the company, but too late to be recorded by the bank.

  deposit ticket   （公司）银行存款明细单

A document showing the firm's name, its account number, and the amount of money deposited into the bank.

  depreciation n.   折旧

The cost of a fixed asset distributed over its entire estimated lifetime.

  discounted notes receivable   （附折扣优惠的）应收票据

A term used to describe notes receivable sold to a bank and being held liable for maturity if the maker defaults.

  dishonored check   空头支票

A check that the bank refuses to pay because the writer does not have sufficient funds in his or her checking account.

  dishonored note   未付（拒付）票据

A note that the maker fails to pay at the time of maturity.

  double-entry accounting   复式记账

An almost universal system that produces equal debit and credit entries for every transaction.

  draft   n.   转付通知

An order by the seller to the buyer stating that the buyer must pay a certain amount of money to a third party.

  drawing n.   业主提取（现金或存货）

The taking of cash or goods out of a business by the owner for personal use. Also known as a withdrawal.

  earnings statement   工资（薪金）明细表

A stub attached to an employee's payroll check that provides the employee with a record of the amount earned and a detailed list of deductions.

  employee n.   员工，雇员

An individual who works for compensation for an employer.

  endorsement n.   背书，签名

The placing of a signature on the back of a check that is to be deposited or cashed.

  endorsement in full   完全背书

A type of endorsement that states that the check can be cashed or transferred only on the order of the person named in the endorsement.

  EOM   月末

Term used to denote the end of the month.

  expenses n.   费用，支出

The decrease in capital caused by the business's revenue-producing operations.

  face of note   票据，凭证的数量

The amount of a note.

  federal unemployment tax   联邦失业保险金

A tax paid by employers only used to supplement state unemployment benefits.

  FICA taxes   联邦保险贡献行为税（社会养老保险金）

Social Security taxes collected in equal amounts from both the employee and the employer. These proceeds are paid into a fund that provides disability and old-age payments. FICA stands for Federal Insurance Contributions Act.

  fiscal period   财政年度，会计期间

A period of time covered by the entire accounting cycle, usually consisting of 12 consecutive months.

  footing n. 合计

The recording in pencil of the temporary total of one side of a T account.

  goodwill n. 商誉

An intangible asset that results from the expectation that the business has the ability to produce an above-average rate of earnings compared to other businesses in the same industry.

  gross pay （员工）毛（工资）收入

The rate, arrived at through negotiation between the employer and the employee, at which employees are paid.

  gross profit 毛利润（营业利润）

Net sales minus cost of goods sold.

  imprest system 预付款方式

A fund established for a fixed petty cash amount and periodically reimbursed by a single check for amounts expended.

  income statement 利润表

A summary of the revenue, expenses, and net income of a business entity for a specific period of time. Also known as a profit and loss statement.

  index number 索引号

Used to compare business activities during one time period with similar activity during another time period.

  interest n. 利息

Money paid for the use or borrowing of money.

  interest-bearing note 票据还本付息允诺书

A note in which the maker has agreed to pay the face of the note plus interest.

  interest rate 利率

A percentage of the principal that is paid for the use of money borrowed.

  journal n. 日记账

The book of original entry for accounting data. It is the book in which the accountant originally records business transactions.

  journalizing n. 记录日记账

A process of recording business transactions in the journal.

  ledger n. 分类账

The complete set of accounts for a business entity. It is used to classify and summarize transactions and to prepare data for financial statements.

| liabilities | n. | 负债 |

Amounts owed to outsiders.

| long-term liabilities | | 长期负债 |

Debts that do not have to be paid immediately but are usually paid over a long period of time, normally more than 1 year.

| loss | n. | 亏损 |

The amount by which total costs exceed total income.

| maker | n. | 付款方 |

An individual who signs a promissory note agreeing to make payment.

| markdown | n. | 降价 |

Downward adjustments of the selling price. Used to induce customers to buy.

| markon | n. | 提价 |

The percent increase in selling price, when cost is used as a base for markup percent.

| markup | n. | 卖价成本差 |

The difference between cost and selling price.

| maturity date | | 票据到期日 |

The date a note is to be paid.

| maturity value | | 票据到期值 |

The face of the note plus interest accrued until the due date.

| median | n. | 中间值 |

The number that divides a group in half.

| merchandise inventory | | 现有存货价值 |

Represents the value of goods on hand, either at the beginning or end of the accounting period.

| merchandise inventory turnover | | 平均存货周转率 |

The number of times the average inventory is sold during a year. This ratio shows how quickly the inventory is moving.

| net purchases | | 购货净额（已减去购货退回） |

All purchases less returns and purchase discounts.

| net sales | | 销售净额（已减去销售退回） |

Total amount of sales minus returns and sales discounts.

| opening entry | | （公司）开办记录 |

An entry made at the time a business is organized to record the assets, liabilities, and capital of the new firm.

| outstanding checks | | 未兑现支票 |

Checks issued by the depositor but not yet presented to the bank for payment.

outstanding stock　　　　　　　　　未兑现（尚为投资人持有的）股票
The number of shares authorized, issued, and in the hands of stockholders.

par value　　　　　　　　　　　　平均价值，正常价值
An arbitrary amount assigned to each share of capital stock of a given class. It has no correlation to the market value or selling price of the stock.

partnership　　n.　　　　　　　　合伙（企业）
An association of two or more persons to carry on as co-owners of a business for profit.

payee　　n.　　　　　　　　　　　收款人，债权人
The individual that is to receive money from a negotiable instrument.

payroll accounting　　　　　　　　工资，薪金支付账目
Accounting for payments of wages, salaries, and related payroll taxes.

payroll earnings card　　　　　　　（员工）工资薪金明细卡
A card that shows payroll data and yearly cumulative earnings, as well as deductions, for each employee.

payroll register　　　　　　　　　工资薪水册
A specially designed form used at the close of each payroll period to summarize and compute the payroll for the period.

payroll tax expense account　　　　工资税金费用账目
An account used for recording the employer's matching portion of the FICA tax and the federal and state unemployment tax.

percent　　n.　　　　　　　　　　百分比
The relationship between one number and another in terms of hundredths.

post-closing trial balance　　　　　结账后验证性试算平衡表
A trial balance made after the closing entries are completed. Only balance sheet items—that is, assets, liabilities, and capital—will appear on this statement.

posting　　n.　　　　　　　　　　过账
The process of transferring information from the journal to the ledger for the purpose of summarizing.

preferred stock　　　　　　　　　优先股
A class of corporate stock that carries certain privileges and rights not given to other shares.

prepaid expenses　　　　　　　　　预付费用
Current assets that represent expenses that have already been paid out, though were not yet consumed during the current period.

present value　　　　　　　　　　现时价值（市场价值）
The face amount of the note plus accrued interest.

proprietorship n. 私营（独资）企业
A business owned by one person.

purchase discount 购货折扣
A cash discount allowed for prompt payment of an invoice.

purchase invoice 购货凭证
The source document prepared by the seller listing the items shipped, their cost, and the method of shipment.

purchase Returns 购货退回
An account used by the buyer to record the reduction granted by the seller for the return of merchandise.

ratio n. 比，比率
The relationship of two or more numbers to each other.

real accounts 实账户
All balance sheet items—that is, assets, liabilities, and capital—having balances that will be carried forward from one period to another.

restrictive endorsement 约束性背书，限制性背书
A type of endorsement that limits the receiver of the check as to the use she or he can make of the funds collected.

revenue n. 总收入，收益
The increase in capital resulting from the delivery of goods or rendering of services by business.

running balance （会计记账的）借贷平衡
The balance of an account after the recording of each transaction.

salary n. 薪水，薪金
Business term used to refer to the compensation for administrative and managerial personnel.

sales discount 销售折扣
A reduction from the original price, granted by the seller to the buyer.

schedule of accounts payable 应付账款明细表
A detailed list of the amounts owed to each creditor.

schedule of accounts receivable 应收账款明细表
A detailed list of the amount due from each customer.

share of stock 股票份额，收益
Represents a unit of the stockholders' interest in the business.

special journal 特种日记账
The book of original entry in which the accountant records specified types of transactions.

state unemployment taxes 国家（政府）失业保险金

Taxes to be paid only by employers, with rates and amounts differing among each state.

  stockholders n.   股东，股份持有者

The owners of the business.

  subscribed shares   已签名允许出售的股份

Shares that a buyer has contracted to purchase at a specific price on a certain date.

  subsidiary ledger   辅助分类账

A group of accounts representing individual subdivisions of a controlling account.

  T account   "T"形账

A form of ledger account that shows only the account title and the debit and credit sides.

  temporary accounts   临时性账户

Consist of revenue, expense, and drawing accounts that will have a zero balance at the end of the fiscal year.

  time clock   考勤记录钟

A clock that stamps an employee's time card to provide a printed record of when the employee arrives for work and departs for the day.

  trade discounts   贸易折扣

This is not a true discount but an adjustment of the price. With it, a business can adjust a price at which it is willing to bill goods without changing the list price in a catalog.

  transaction n.   交易，业务

An event recorded in the accounting records that can be expressed in terms of money.

  treasury stock   基金（证券的一种）

Stock representing shares that have been issued and later reacquired by the corporation.

  trial balance   试算平衡表

A two-column schedule that compares the total of all debit balances with the total of all credit balances.

  Uniform Partnership Act   合伙（争端）调解决议，法案

A law used to resolve all contested matters among partners of a partnership.

  unissued shares   未发行股份

Authorized shares that have not been offered for sale.

  unlimited liability   无限责任

The right of creditors to claim any and all assets of a debtor in satisfaction of claims held against the business of the debtor.

  worksheet n.   工作底稿

An informal accounting statement that summarizes the trial balance and other information necessary to prepare financial statements.

Appendix 3

Key to Exercises

（练习参考答案）

Chapter 1

 Summary

1. Accounting; 2. generally accepted accounting principles (GAAP); 3. Assets, Liabilities, Capital (Owners' Equity); 4. assets; 5. Capital; 6. liability; 7. capital; 8. assets, capital; 9. liability; 10. cash; 11. capital; 12. capital; 13. transaction; 14. in balance; 15. Revenue, Expenses.

 Solved Problems

1. (1) ② ④ ⑥ ⑧ (2) ⑤ (3) ① ③ ⑦
2. (1) $51,500   (2) $52,750   (3) $19,000   (4) $12,700   (5) $12,000   (6) $14,400
3. (1) No effect—only the asset (machinery) and liability are affected (accounts payable).
   (2) No effect—the same reason.
   (3) Decrease in capital—capital is withdrawn.
   (4) Increase in capital—fees are income that increases capital.
   (5) No effect –the asset cash is decreased while the asset supplies is increased.
   (6) Decrease in capital—supplies that are used represent an expense (reduction in capital).
4. The accounting equation is: Assets = Liabilities + Owner's Equity. Therefore, if assets increased by $20,000 and liabilities increased by $12,000, owner's equity must have increased by $8,000, as indicated in the following computation:

$$\text{Assets} = \text{Liabilities} + \text{Capital}$$
$$+\$20,000 = +\$12,000 + \text{Capital}$$
$$+\$20,000 - \$12,000 = \text{Capital}$$
$$+\$8,000 = \text{Capital}$$

5. Assets = Liabilities + Capital
    (1) I   NE   I
    (2) NE   NE   NE
    (3) I   I   NE
    (4) D   D   NE
    (5) I   I   NE
    (6) I   NE   I
    (7) D   NE   D

6.   Assets   =   Liabilities + Capital
            $8,600
            4,000
            12,000
            $24,600 = $5,000   + $19,600

7.   Assets   =   Liabilities   +   Capital
         Cash   Equipment   Notes Payable
Balance $15,000 $15,000
Entry   −3,000 + $14,000 $11,000*   _____
Balance $12,000 + $14,000 $11,000   + $15,000

* Total value of auto $14,000
   Less cash deposit   3,000
   Amount owed $11,000

8.   Assets   =   Liabilities   +   Capital
                Supplies
Balance
  (Beginning of month) $6,400   + $6,400
Entry   −4,200   −4,200 Supplies Expense
Balance $2,200 $2,200
  (End of month)

Supplies is an asset. Supplies expense ($4,200) represents the amount that has been used. This amount is applied as a reduction in capital.

9. The owner's equity of Coca-Cola is $9,513.

The owner's equity of PepsiCo is $6,881.

10. (1) Invested cash, supplies, and machinery into the firm.
    (2) Bought additional supplies for cash.
    (3) Bought a $9,000 machine, paying $2,000 down and owing the balance.
    (4) Income for the period.
    (5) Paid salaries expense.
    (6) Supplies inventory was determined.
    (7) Paid in full amount owed (see transaction 3).
    (8) Owner withdrew cash for personal use.

11.

	Assets			=	Liabilities	+	Capital	
	Cash	+ Supplies	+ Equipment		Accounts Payable		Rag Time Band Co.	
(1)	$22,000						$22,000	
(2)	−4,000		+$10,000		+$6,000			
Balance	$18,000		$10,000	=	$6,000		+ $22,000	
(3)	−500	+ $500						
Balance	$17,500 +	$500	+ $10,000	=	$6,000		+ $22,000	
(4)	+3,000						+ 3,000	Fees Income
Balance	$20,500 +	$500	+ $10,000	=	$6,000		+ $25,000	
(5)	−1,200						−1,200	Salaries Expense
Balance	$19,300 +	$500	+ $10,000	=	$6,000		+ $23,800	
(6)	−600						−600	General Expense
Balance	$18,700 +	$500	+ $10,000	=	$6,000		+ $23,200	
(7)	−1,000				−1,000			
Balance	$17,700 +	$500	+ $10,000	=	$5,000		+ $23,200	
(8)		−300					−300	Supplies Expense
Balance	$17,700 +	$200	+ $10,000	=	$5,000		+ $22,900	

12.

	Assets				=	Liabilities	+	Capital
	Cash	+ Supplies	+ Equipment	+ Land		Accounts Payable		Capital, R. Lawn
Jan. 1	$5,000		$4,500					$9,500
Jan. 4		+$750				+$750		
Balance	$5,000	$750	$4,500		=	$750		$9,500

Date	Cash	Supplies	Equipment	=	Accounts Payable	Capital	
Jan. 9	−300					−300	Rent Expense
Balance	$4,700	$750	$4,500	=	$750	$9,200	
Jan. 15	+1,100					+1,100	Fees Earned
Balance	$5,800	$750	$4,500	=	$750	$10,300	
Jan. 17	−1,900					−1,900	Salaries Expense
Balance	$3,900	$750	$4,500	=	$750	$8,400	
Jan. 21	−1,000		+1,000				
Balance	$2,900	$750	$1,000	$4,500	=	$750	$8,400
Jan. 24	−500				−500		
Balance	$2,400	$750	$1,000	$4,500	=	$250	$8,400
Jan. 27	−500					−500	Drawing
Balance	$1,900	$750	$1,000	$4,500	=	$250	$7,900
Jan. 29	−1,500			+1,500			
Balance	$400	$750	$1,000	$6,000	=	$250	$7,900
Jan. 31		−350				−350	Supplies Expense
Balance	$400	$400	$1,000	$6,000	=	$250	$7,550

13.   **Assets** = **Liabilities** + **Capital**

	Cash	+ Supplies	+ Equipment	Accounts Payable	B. Glatt, Capital	
(1)	$14,000		$6,000		$20,000	
(2)			+2,000	+$2,000		
Balance	$14,000 +	+	$8,000	= $2,000 +	$20,000	
(3)	−600 +	$600				
Balance	$13,400 +	$600 +	$8,000	= $2,000 +	$20,000	
(4)	−500			−500		
Balance	$12,900 +	$600 +	$8,000	= $1,500 +	$20,000	
(5)	+2,400			+	2,400	Fees Income
Balance	$15,300 +	$600 +	$8,000	= $1,500 +	$22,400	
(6)	−300				−300	Salaries Expense
Balance	$15,000 +	$600 +	$8,000	= $1,500 +	$22,100	
(7)	−400				−400	Gerneral Expense
Balance	$14,600 +	$600 +	$8,000	= $1,500 +	$21,700	
(8)	−1,500			−1,500		
Balance	$13,100 +	$600 +	$8,000	= — +	$21,700	
(9)	−700				−700	Drawing

Balance	$12,400	+ $600	+ $8,000	=	—	+	$21,000	
(10)	–450						–450	Supplies Expense
Balance	$12,400	+ $600	+ $8,000	=	—	+	$20,550	

14.

	Assets			=	Liabilities	+	Capital	
	Cash	+ Supplies	+ Automobiles		Accounts Payable		Capital	
Balance	$6,400	+ $800	+ $4,500		$2,000	+	$9,700	
(1)	–2,000				–2,000			
Balance	$4,400	+ $800	+ $4,500	=	$—	+	$9,700	
(2)	+8,200						+8,200	Fee Income
Balance	$12,600	+ $800	+ $4,500	=	$—	+	$17,900	
(3)	–1,900						–1,900	Wages Expense
Balance	$10,700	+ $800	+ $4,500	=	$—	+	$16,000	
(4)	–200						–200	Advertising Expense
Balance	$10,500	+ $800	+ $4,500	=	$—	+	$15,800	
(5)	–2,500		+5,000		+$2,500			
Balance	$8,000	+ $800	+ $9,500	=	$2,500	+	$15,800	
(6)	–425						–425	Maintenance Expense
Balance	$7,575	+ $800	+ $9,500	=	$2,500	+	$15,375	
(7)	+100	–100						
Balance	$7,675	+ $700	+ $9,500	=	$2,500	+	$15,375	
(8)	–800						–800	Drawing
Balance	$6,875	+ $700	+ $9,500	=	$2,500	+	$14,575	
(9)		–350					–350	Supplies Expense
Balance	$6,875	+ $350	+ $9,500	=	$2,500	+	$14,225	

Chapter 2

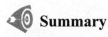
Summary

1. account; 2. double-entry accounting; 3. ledger; 4. debit side, credit side; 5. debited; 6. credited; 7. credited; 8. credited; 9. debited; 10. capital; 11. trial balance.

Solved Problems

1.

Assets	
Dr.	Cr.
+	−

Liabilities	
Dr.	Cr.
−	+

Capital	
Dr.	Cr.
−	+

Income	
Dr.	Cr.
−	+

Expense	
Dr.	Cr.
+	−

2.

Accounts	Designated number
Cash	11
Accounts Receivable	12
Equipment	17
Accounts Payable	21
Notes Payable	22
Capital	31
Drawing	32
Fees Income	41
Rent Expense	51
Miscellaneous Expense	59

3. (1) Cr.   (2) Cr.   (3) Cr.   (4) Dr.   (5) Dr.   (6) Cr.   (7) Dr.

4.

	Dr.	Cr.
(1)	(3)	(2)
(2)	(8)	(3)
(3)	(3)	(6)
(4)	(9)	(3)
(5)	(5)	(1)
(6)	(1)	(3)
(7)	(10)	(1)
(8)	(3)	(7)
(9)	(11)	(10)
(10)	(4)	(3)

Appendix 3 Key to Exercises（练习参考答案）

5.

(1) Supplies	Cash	Accounts Payable
600	Bal. 2,000	600

(2) Equipment	Cash	Accounts Payable
2,700	Bal. 1,000 | 900	1,800

(3) Accounts Payable	Notes Payable
1,800 | 1,800 Bal.	1,800

(4) Cash	Fees Income
500	500

6.

	Transaction	Account Debited	Effect of Debit	Account Credited	Effect of Credit
(1)	Invested $14,000 in firm	Cash	Increased asset	Capital	Increased Capital
(2)	Bought $10,000 of equipment of cash	Equipment	Increased asset	Cash	Decreased asset
(3)	Bought $6,000 of additional equipment on account	Equipment	Increased asset	Accounts Payable	Increased liability
(4)	Paid $200 for supplies	Supplies	Increased asset	Cash	Decreased asset
(5)	Received $1,000 in fees	Cash	Increased asset	Fees Income	Increased income
(6)	Paid $300 for salaries	Salaries Expense	Increased expense	Cash	Decreased asset
(7)	Paid $500 for rent	Rent Expense	Increased expense	Cash	Decreased asset
(8)	Withdrew $100 for personal use	Drawing	Decreased Capital	Cash	Decreased asset
(9)	Paid $2,000 on account	Accounts Payable	Decreased liability	Cash	Decreased asset
(10)	Paid $300 for gasoline	Gasoline Expense	Increased expense	Cash	Decreased asset

7.

	Dr.	Cr.
Cash	$20,000	
Accounts Receivable	14,000	
Supplies	6,000	
Equipment	18,000	
Accounts Payable		$ 9,000
Notes Payable		11,000
P. Henry, Capital		32,000
P. Henry, Drawing	4,000	
Fees Income		26,000
Salaries Expense	8,000	
Rent Expense	5,000	
Supplies Expense	2,000	
General Expense	1,000	
	$78,000	$78,000

8.

M. Ramirez

Trial Balance

January 31, 200X

	Dr.	Cr.
Cash	$29,000	
Accounts Receivable	4,000	
Accounts Payable		$3,000
Capital		12,500
Drawing	500	
Fees Income		33,000
Rent Expense	1,000	
Salaries Expense	0,000	
General Expense	4,000	
	$48,500	$48,500

9.

P. Johnson
Trial Balance
December 31, 200X

	Dr.	Cr.
Cash	$2,700	
Accounts Receivable	11,400	
Supplies	800	
Equipment	18,500	
Accounts Payable		$1,500
Notes Payable		
Johnson, Capital		15,400
Johnson, Drawing	500	
Fees Income		29,000
Salaries Expense	8,000	
Rent Expense	3,000	
Supplies Expense	200	
General Expense	800	
	$45,900	$45,900

10.

Cash			
(1)	14,000	600	(3)
(5)	2,400	500	(4)
12,400	16,400	300	(6)
		400	(7)
		1,500	(8)
		700	(9)
		4,000	

Equipment	
(1)	6,000
(2)	2,000
	8,000

Fees Income	
	2,400 (5)

Accounts Payable			
(4)	500	2,000	(2)
(8)	1,500		

Supplies Expense	
(10) 450	

Capital	
	20,000 (1)

Salaries Expense	
(6) 300	

Supplies			
(3)	600	450	(10)
150			

Drawing	
(9) 700	

General Expense	
(7) 400	

B. Glatt
Trial Balance
December 31, 200X

Cash	$12,400	
Supplies	250	
Equipment	8,000	
Capital		$20,000
Drawing	700	
Fees Income		2,400
Supplies Expense	450	
Salaries Expense	300	
General Expense	400	
	$22,400	$22,400

11.

```
         Cash                      Equipment              Cleaning Income
(1)  12,000 | 220   (2)       (3)  3,500 |                        | 1,850  (5)
(5)   1,850 | 1500  (3)
      13,850| 425   (4)
10,830      | 375   (6)       Accounts Payable              Rent Expense
            | 500   (7)       (7)  500 | 2,000  (2)       (4)  425 |
            | 3,020                    | 1,500

        Supplies                     Capital               Salaries Expense
(2)   220   | 60    (8)                  | 12,000  (1)    (6)  375 |
      160

                                                          Supplies Expense
                                                          (8)   60 |
```

12.

Nu-Look Dry Cleaning Company
Trial Balance
November 30, 200X

Cash	$10,830	
Supplies	160	

		(continued)
Equipment	3,500	
Accounts Payable		$1,500
Nu-Look Dry Cleaning Company, Capital		12,000
Cleaning Income		1,850
Rent Expense	425	
Salaries Expense	375	
Supplies Expense	60	
	$15,350	$15,350

Chapter 3

 Summary

1. journal;   2. journal;   3. ledger;   4. journalizing;   5. Source Documents: 6. posting.

 Questions

1. The journals can be grouped into general journals and special journals.
2. There are cash receipts journal, cash disbursements journal, purchases journal and sales journal.
3. Recording a business transaction in a journal (journalizing) includes two steps: (1) Analyze transactions from source documents; (2) Record transactions in a journal under the double-entry system.
4. Posting is ordinarily carried out in the following steps: (1) Record the amount and date; (2) Record the posting reference in the account; (3) Record the posting in the journal.

 Solved Problems

1.

		Debit	Credit
(1)	Equipment	10,000	
	Cash		2,000
	Accounts Payable, William Smith		8,000
	Purchase of equipment, 20% for cash, balance on account		

(continued)

		Debit	Credit
(2)	Accounts Payable, William Smith	8,000	
	Notes Payable		8,000
	Notes Payable in settlement of accounts payable		
(3)	Notes Payable	8,000	
	Cash		8,000
	Settlement of the notes payable		

2.

	Debit	Credit
Cash	1,2000	
Supplies	1,400	
Equipment	22,600	
Furniture	10,000	
R. Berg, Capital		46,000

3.

	Debit	Credit
Cash	1,2000	
Supplies	1,400	
Equipment	22,600	
Furniture	10,000	
Accounts Payable		3,500
R. Berg, Capital		42,500

4.

		Debit	Credit
(1)	Cash	10,000	
	Stephenson, Capital		10,000
(2)	Office Furniture	2,000	
	Cash		2,000
(3)	Equipment	6,000	
	Accounts Payable		6,000
(4)	Cash	2,200	

		Debit	Credit
	Cleaning Income		2,200
(5)	Accounts Payable	1,500	
	Cash		1,500

(continued)

5.

		Debit	Credit
(1)	Cash	18,000	
	Supplies	4,800	
	Equipment	12,200	
	Accounts Payable		7,000
	Gavis, Capital		28,000
(2)	Cash	2,400	
	Fees Income		2,400
(3)	Cash	5,000	
	Gavis, Capital		5,000
(4)	Accounts Payable	3,500	
	Cash		3,500

6.

		Debit	Credit
(1)	Accounts Receivable	2,400	
	Fees Income		2,400
	To record services rendered on account		
(2)	Cash	1,000	
	Accounts Receivable		1,000
	Received cash on account		

Note: Fees Income had already been recorded in the previous month, when the service had been the rendered. On the accrual basis, income as well as expense is recorded in the period of service or use, not in the period of payment.

7.

General Journal

Date	Description	P. R.	Debit	Credit
Jan. 1	Cash		5,000	
	Equipment		4,100	
	Capital			9,100
12	Rent Expense		400	
	Cash			400
13	Supplies		700	
	Accounts Payable			700
16	Cash		1,700	
	Cleaning Fees			1,700
19	Supplies		550	
	Cash			550
21	Accounts Payable		500	
	Cash			500
22	Utilities Expense		275	
	Cash			275
23	Drawing		500	
	Cash			500
25	Cash		1,100	
	Cleaning Fees			1,100
26	Equipment		900	
	Cash			900
28	Accounts Receivable		500	
	Cleaning Fees			500
30	Cash		300	

		Accounts Receivable			300
	30	Accounts Payable		200	
		Cash			200

8.

Cash					Equipment			Accounts payable		
(1)	9,000	4,000	(2)	(2)	8,000		(3)	3,000	4,000	(2)
(4)	1,500	3,000	(3)	(3)						
		600	(5)							

Charles, Capital			Fares Income			Salaries Expense	
	9,000	(1)		1,500	(4)	(5) 600	

9.

Charles Taxi Company
Trial Balance

Cash	$2,900	
Equipment	8,000	
Accounts Payable		$1,000
Charles, Capital		9,000
Fares Income		1,500
Salaries Expense	600	
	$11,500	$11,500

10. From the T accounts below, prepare a trial balance.

Cash			Capital		Drawing	
10,000	1,000			15,500	1,000	
5,000				2,000		
6,000						
500						

Rent Expense			Accounts Payable		Notes Payable	
500		500	500			1,000
			600			500
			1,000			

Equipment		Land		Accounts Receivable	
2,500		5,000		500	500
		5,000			
		200			

Supplies		Fees Income		Wages Expense	
300			7,000	1,450	
150			9,000		

Ace Hardware Store
Trial Balance
December 31, 200X

Cash	$20,500	
Accounts Receivable	5,200	
Supplies	450	
Land	5,000	
Equipment	2,500	
Accounts Payable		$1,600
Notes Payable		1,500
Capital		17,500
Drawing	1,000	
Fees Income		16,000
Rent Expense	500	
Wages Expense	1,450	
	$36,600	$36,600

11.

Journal   **Page J-6**

	Date	Description	P. R.	Debit	Credit
	200X				
(1)	Nov.2	Notes Payable	22	1,000	
		Cash	11		1,000
		Payment of installment note			
(2)	8	Accounts Payable	21	3,000	
		Cash	11		3,000

					(continued)
		Payment on outstanding accounts			
(3)	15	Cash	11	8,400	
		Admissions Income	41		8,400
		Receipts for the 2-week period to date			
(4)	22	Equipment	17	15,500	
		Cash	11		5,000
		Accounts Payable	21		10,500
		Purchase of a projector with cash			
		payment, balance due in 1 year			
(5)	30	Salaries Expense	51	1,600	
		Cash	11		1,600
		Salaries paid to employees			

```
        Cash           11              Equipment     17            Notes Payable    22
  Bal.  2,400  | J-6  1,000  (1)     Bal.  11,200 |              (1)J-6  1,000 | Bal. 12,000
(3) J-6 8,400  | J-6  3,000  (2)  (4)J-6  15,500  |
    J-6 5,000 (4)|
               | J-6  1,600  (5)

   Accounts Receivable  12              Building    18          Dampman, Capital  31
  Bal.  1,500 |                     Bal.  10,000 |                              | Bal. 4,000


       Supplies         14           Accounts Payable  21         Admission Income 41
  Bal.   350  |                    (2) J-6  3,000 | Bal.   9,450 |            | J-6  8,400 (3)
                                                  | J-6   10,500 (4)

                                                                   Salaries Expense  51
                                                                (5) J-6  1,600 |
```

Dampman Playhouse
Trial Balance
November 30, 200X

Cash	$200	
Accounts Receivable	1,500	
Supplies	350	
Equipment	26,700	
Building	10,000	
Accounts Payable		$16,950
Notes Payable		11,000
Dampman, Capital		4,000
Admissions Income		8,400
Salaries Expense	1,600	
	$40,350	$40,350

Chapter 4

Summary

1. accounting statement;   2.income;   3.income;   4.income, expense;   5.net income;   6.capital;   7.capital;   8.assets, liabilities, capital;   9.liabilities and capital;   10.year or period.

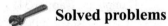
Solved problems

1. (1) 12,090;   (2) $73,450
2. There are two steps to solving this problem:
   (1) Prepare an income statement.
   (2) Determine increases or decreases in capital by subtracting the drawing (withdrawal) from the net income.

Fees Income		$14,000
Expenses		
Rent Expense	$2,000	
Salaries Expense	5,000	
Miscellaneous Expense	1,000	

		(continued)
Total Expenses		8,000
Net Income		$6,000
Net Income	6,000	
Less: Drawing	2,000	
Increase in Capital	$4,000	

3. If the withdrawal is larger than the net income, a decrease in capital will result.

New Income	$6,000
Drawing	9,000
Decease in Capital	$3,000

4.

	Income Statement		Balance Sheet		
	Income	Expense	Assets	Liability	Capital
Accounts Payable				√	
Accounts Receivable			√		
Building			√		
Capital					√
Cash			√		
Drawing					√
Equipment			√		
Fees Income	√				
General Expense		√			
Interest Expense		√			
Interest Income	√				
Land			√		
Notes Payable				√	
Other Income	√				
Rent Expense		√			
Rent Income	√				
Salaries Expense		√			
Supplies			√		
Supplies Expense		√			
Tax Expense		√			

5.

ASSETS		
Cash		$4,000
Supplies		200
Equipment		16,000
Total Assets		$20,200
LIABILITIES AND CAPITAL	$3,000	
Accounts Payable	12,000	
Notes Payable		$15,000
Total Liabilities		5,200
Capital, December 31, 200X *		$20,200
***CAPITAL STATEMENT**		
Capital, January 1, 200X		$4,000
Net Income	$11,400	
Less: Drawing	10,200	
Increase in Capital		1,200
Capital, December 31, 200X		$5,200

6.

	Current Asset	Fixed Asset	Current Liability	Long-Term Liability
Accounts Receivable	√			
Accounts Payable			√	
Note Payable			√	
Mortgage Payable				√
Cash	√			
Supplies	√			
Salaries Payable			√	
Bonds Payable				√
Equipment		√		
Land		√		

7. (1)

R. Dames

Income Statement

Year Ended December 31, 200X

Admissions Income		$34,200

(continued)

Expenses		
Film Rental Expense	$6,000	
Rent Expense	10,000	
Salaries Expense	7,000	
Miscellaneous Expense	4,000	
Total Expenses		27,000
Net Income		$7,200

(2) The capital statement is needed to show the capital balance at the end of the year. Mr. Dames' capital balance above is at the beginning. Net income increases capital, and drawing reduces capital.

R. Dames

Capital Statement

Year Ended December 31, 200X

Capital, January 1, 200X		$16,000
Add: Net Income	$7,200	
Less: Drawing	5,400	
Increase in Capital		1,800
Capital, December 31, 200X		$17,800

(3)

R. Dames

Balance Sheet

Year Ended December 31, 200X

ASSETS		
Cash	$7,500	
Supplies	4,200	
Equipment	18,500	$30,200
Total Assets		
LIABILITIES AND CAPITAL		
Accounts Payable	$11,400	
Notes Payable	1,000	
Total Liabilities		$12,400
Capital		17,800
Total Liabilities and Capital		$30,200

Chapter 5

Summary

1. accrual basis; 2. insurance expense; 3. asset, balance sheet, expense, income statement;
4. liability account, expense account; 5. deductions; 6. Accounts Receivable, Equipment;
7. Prepaid Expense; 8. Expense and Income Summary; 9. Capital; 10. asset, liability, capital

Solved Problems

1.

(1)	Salaries Expense	4,000	
	Salaries Payable		4,000
(2)	Salaries Expense	8,000	
	Salaries Payable		8,000

2.

| Insurance Expense | 50# | |
| Prepaid Insurance | | 50 |

$600/2 years × 2/12 months = $50

3.

| Office Supplies Expense | 400 | |
| Office Supplies | | 400 |

4.

| Depreciation Expense—Machinery | 100# | |
| Accumulated Depreciation—Machinery | | 100 |

#$12,000 × 10% per year × 1/12 year = $100

5.

| Depreciation | 3,000 | |
| Accumulated Depreciation | | 3,000 |

((cost − salvage value) / depreciation period) × months in use = ($60,000 − 0) / 60 months = $3,000

6.

Salaries Expense	1,000	
Salaries Payable		1,000

$500 × 2 = $1,000

7.

(1)

Insurance Expense	1,500	
Prepaid Insurance		1,500

$9,000 / 36 months = $250 × 6 months = $1,500

(2)

Prepaid Insurance	7,500	
Insurance Expense		7,500

$9,000 / 36 months × 30 months = $7,500

Note that here we are concerned with how much is left of the policy amount.

8.

(1)

Supplies Expense	850	
Supplies		850

$2,000 − $1,150 = $850

(2)

Supplies	1,500	
Supplies Expense		1,500

9.

(1) $1,200

(2) $2,400 ($4,000 / 5 days = $800 per day; $800 × 3 days = $2,400)

(3) $480 ($650 − $170)

(4) $200

10.

Adjusting Entries

(1)	Supplies Expense	520	
	Supplies		520

			(continued)
(2)	Depreciation Expense	900	
	Accumulated Depreciation		900
(3)	Wages Expense	725	
	Wages Payable		725
(4)	Utilities Expense	215	
	Accounts Payable		215
(5)	Insurance Expense	1,150	
	Prepaid Insurance		1,150
(6)	Cash	2,175	
	Sales Income		2,175

Cash	Accounts Receivable	Supplies	Accounts Payable
7,555	1,750	915 | 520 (1)	975
(6) 2,175			215 (4)

D. Money, Capital	Wages Expense	Prepaid Insurance	Fees Income
17,000	20,665	1,575 | 1,150 (5)	16,450
	(3) 725		2,175 (6)

Utilities Expense	Supplies Expense	Depreciation Expense	Accumulated Depreciation
715	(1) 520	(2) 900	900 (2)
(4) 215			

Wages Payable	Insurance Expense	D. Money, Drawing	
725 (3)	(5) 1,150	1,250	

11.

Closing Entries

(1)	Fees Income	28,625	
	Expense and Income Summary		28,625
(2)	Expense and Income Summary	24,890	
	Wages Expense		21,390
	Insurance Expense		1,150
	Depreciation Expense		900
	Supplies Expense		520
	Utilities Expense		930
(3)	Expense and Income Summary	3,735	
	D. Money, Capital		3,735
(4)	Expense and Income Summary	1,250	
	D. Money, Drawing		1,250

12.

(1)	Salaries Expense	5,000	
	Salaries Payable		5,000
(2)	Expense and Income Summary	205,000	
	Salaries Expense		205,000

13.

Insurance Expense	200	
Prepaid Insurance		200
Supplies Expense	240	
Supplies		240
Depreciation Expense	1,800	
Accumulated Depreciation		1,800
Salaries Expense	4,000	
Salaries Payable		4,000

14.

	(1)	Fees Income	12,000	
		Expense and Income Summary		12,000
	(2)	Expense and Income Summary	6,240	
		Salaries Expense		4,000
		Insurance Expense		200
		Depreciation Expense		1,800
		Supplies Expense		240
	(3)	Expense and Income Summary	5,760	
		Capital		5,760

15.

Post Closing Trial Balance

Account	Dr.	Cr.
Cash	36,860	
Prepaid Insurance	400	
Supplies	300	
Equipment	6,000	
Accumulated Depreciation		1,800
Salaries Payable		4,000
Capital		37,760
	43,560	43,560

16.

	(1)	Service Income	10,000	
		Interest Income	2,000	
		Expense and Income Summary		12,000
	(2)	Expense and Income Summary	10,000	
		Salaries Expense		6,000
		Rent Expense		2,000
		Depreciation Expense		1,500
		Interest Expense		500

17.

| Expense and Income Summary | 2,000 | |
| Capital | | 2,000 |

```
    Expense and Income Summary                  Capital
(2)  10,000  | 12,000  (1)                            | Bal. 20,000
(3)   2,000  |                                        |      2,000 (3)
     ------- | -------
     12,000  | 12,000
```

18.

Expense and Income Summary	50,000	
Laura Anthony, Capital		50,000
Laura Anthony, Capital	35,000	
Laura Anthony, Drawing		35,000

19.

(1)	Service Income	12,000	
	Interest Income	1,500	
	Expense and Income Summary		13,500
(2)	Expense and Income Summary	17,000	
	Wages and Salaries Expense		8,000
	Rent Expense		4,000
	Depreciation Expense		3,000
	Interest Expense		2,000
(3)	P. Silvergold, Capital	3,500	
	Expense and Income Summary		3,500
(4)	P. Silvergold, Capital	6,000	
	P. Silvergold, Drawing		6,000

$3,500 represents a net loss and is debited to the capital account.

Appendix 4

资产负债表（一） 会外工 01 表
年　　月　　日　　　　FORM AFI-01
BALANCE SHEET　单位：人民币
AT　　20　　　　MONETARY UNIT: RMB ¥

资产 ASSETS	行次 LINE	年初数 Bal. B/Y	期末数 Bal. E/P	负债及所有者权益 LIABILITES AND CAPITAL	行次 LINE	年初数 Bal. B/Y	期末数 Bal. E/P
流动资产： CURRENT ASSETS				流动负债： CURRENT LIABILITIES			
现金 Cash on hand				短期借款 Short term loans			
备用金 Pretty cash				应付票据 Notes payable			
银行存款 Cash in banks				应付账款 Accounts payable			
有价证券 Marketable receivable				内部往来 Inter-company accounts			
应收票据 Notes receivable				预收货款 Items received in advance-supplied			
应收账款 Accounts receivable				应付工资 Accrued payroll			
贷：坏账准备 Less: allowance for bad debts				应交税金 Taxes payable			
预付货款 Prepayments——supplies				应付股利 Dividends payable			
内部往来 Inter-company accounts				其他应付款 Other payable			
				预提费用 Accrued expenses			
其他应收款 Other receivables				职工奖励及福利基金 Bonds and welfare funds			

(续表)

资产 ASSETS	行次 LINE	年初数 Bal. B/Y	期末数 Bal. E/P	负债及所有者权益 LIABILITES AND CAPITAL	行次 LINE	年初数 Bal. B/Y	期末数 Bal. E/P
待摊费用 Prepaid and deferred expenses				一年内到期的长期负债 Matured long term liabilities within a year			
存货 Inventories				其他流动负债 Other current liabilities			
存货变现损失准备 less: allowance on inventory reduction to market				流动负债合计 Total current liabilities			
转未完工生产成本 Transferred in production cost transforming				长期负债： LONG TERM LIABILITIES			
一年内到期的长期投资 Matured long time investments within a year				长期借款： Long term loans			
流动资产合计 Total current assets				应付公司债 Bonds payable			
长期投资： LONG TERM INVESTMENT				应付公司债溢价（折价） Premium on bonds payable (discount)			
长期投资： Long term investment				一年以上的应付款项 Accounts payable over a year			
				长期负债合计： Total long term liabilities			
一年以上的应收款项 Account receivable over a year				其他负债： OTHER LIABILITIES			
固定资产： FIXED ASSETS				筹建期间汇兑收益 Exchange gains during organization period			
固定资产原价 Fixed assets——cost				递延投资收益 Deferred investment gains			

(续表)

资产 ASSETS	行次 LINE	年初数 Bal. B/Y	期末数 Bal. E/P	负债及所有者权益 LIABILITES AND CAPITAL	行次 LINE	年初数 Bal. B/Y	期末数 Bal. E/P
减：累计折旧 Less: accumulated depreciation				递延税款贷项 Credit side of deferred tax			
固定资产净值 Fixed assets——net value				其他递延贷项 Credit side of other tax			
固定资产清理 Disposal of fixed assets				待转销汇兑收益 Prepaid and deferred exchange profit			
				其他负债合计 Total other liabilities			
				负债合计 Total liabilities			

资产负债表（二）

会外工 01 表
FORM AFI-01

BALANCE SHEET

年　　月　　日
AT　　　　20

单位：人民币
MONETARY UNIT: RMB ￥

资产 ASSETS	行次 LINE	年初数 Bal. B/Y	期末数 Bal. E/P	负债及所有者权益 LIABILITES AND CAPITAL	行次 LINE	年初数 Bal. B/Y	期末数 Bal. E/P
融资租入固定资产原价 Fixed assets—cost on financial lease				所有者权益 Investor's equity			
减：融资租入固定资产折旧 Less: accumulated depreciation				资本总额（货币名称及金额） Authorized capital( )			
融资租入固定资产净值 Fixed assets—cost on financial lease				实收资本（外币金额期末数） Paid in capital( )			
在建工程： CONSTRUCTION WORK IN PROCESS				其中： Including			
在建工程 Construction work in process				中方投资（外币金额期末数） Chinese investment( )			
在建工程 Construction work in process				外方投资（外币金额期末数） Foreign investment( )			
无形资产： INTANGIBLE ASSETS				减：已归还投资 Less: returned investments			
场地使用权 Right to the use of a site				资本公积 Accumulation of capital			
工业产权及专有技术 Industrial property right and patents				公司拨入资金 Funds from head office			
其他无形资产 Other intangibles				储备基金 Reserve funds			
无形资产合计 Total intangibles assets				企业发展工基金 Expansion funds			

（续表）

资产 ASSETS	行次 LINE	年初数 Bal. B/Y	期末数 Bal. E/P	负债及所有者权益 LIABILITES AND CAPITAL	行次 LINE	年初数 Bal. B/Y	期末数 Bal. E/P
其他资产： OTHER ASSETS				利润归还投资 Investment returned with profit			
开办费 Organization expenses				本年利润 Current profit			
筹建期间汇兑损失 Exchange losses darning organization period				未分配利润 Retained earning			
递延投资损失 Deferred investment losses				货币换算金额 Currency translation difference			
递延税款借项 Debt side of deferred tax							
其他递延支出 Other deferred expenditures							
待转销汇兑损益 Prepaid and deferred exchange loss							
其他递延借项 Debit side of other deferred							
其他资产合计 Total other assets				所有者权益合计 Total investor's equity			
资产合计 TOTAL ASSETS				负债及所有者权益合计 TOTAL LIABILITIES AND INVESTORS EQUITY			

附注：1. 委托加工材料 元 2. 受托代销商品 元
3. 代管商品物资 元 4. 由企业负责的应收票据贴现 元
5. 租入固定资产 元 6. 本年支付的进口环节税金

Notes: 1. materials processed on commission ￥ 2. Goods in consignment ￥

3. Goods held in our custody ￥ 4. Contingent Liability incurred by discounted receivable ￥

5. Leasehold fixed asset ￥ 6. Import tax paid this year ￥

7. Bal: Balance; B/Y: Beginning of Year; E/P: End of Period

8. Monetary unit and amount: 9. Amount: of foreign currency at end of period

现金流量表（一）

Cash Flows Statement

年度　　会外 03 表　　FORM AF-03
For the period ended　　单位：人民币 元
Monetary Unit: RMB ￥

项　　目	Items	行次 NO.	金额 Amount
一．经营活动产生的现金流量	**Cash Flows from Operating Activities**		
销售商品提供劳务收到的现金	Cash received from sales of goods or rendering of services	1	
收到的租金	Rental received	2	
收到的增值税销项税额和退回的增值税款	Value added tax on sales received and refunds of value added tax paid	3	
收到的除增值税以外的其他税费返还	Refund of tax and levy other than value added tax	4	
收到的其他与经营活动有关的现金	Other cash received relating to operating activities	7	
现金流入小计	Sub-total of cash in flows	8	
购买商品接受劳务支付的现金	Cash paid for goods and services	9	
经营租赁所支付的现金	Cash paid for operating leases	10	
支付给职工以及为职工支付的现金	Cash paid to and on behalf of employees	11	
支付的增值税款	Value added tax on purchases paid	12	
支付的所得税款	Income tax paid	13	
支付的除增值税所得税以外的其他税费	Taxes paid other than value added tax and income tax	14	
支付的其他与经营活动有关的现金	Other cash received relating to operating activities	17	
现金流出小计	**Sub-total of cash outflows**	18	
经营活动产生的现金流量净额	**Net cash flows from Investing activities**	19	

（续表）

项　　目	Items	行次 NO.	金额 Amount
二．投资活动产生的现金流量	Cash Flows from Investing Activities		
收回投资收到的现金	Cash received from of return investments	20	
分得股利或利润所收到的现金	Cash received from distribution of dividends or profits	21	
取得债券利息收入所收到的现金	Cash received form bond interest income	22	
处置固定资产、无形资产和其他长期资产而收到的现金净额	Net cash received from disposal of fixed assets, intangible assets and other long-term assets	23	
收到的其他与投资活动有关的现金	Other cash received relating to investing activities	26	
现金流入小计	Sub-total of cash inflows	27	
购建固定资产，无形资产和其他长期资产所支付的现金	Cash paid to acquire fixed assets, intangible assets and other long-term assets	28	
权益性投资所支付的现金	Cash paid to acquire equity investments	29	
债权性投资所支付的现金	Cash paid to acquire debt investment	30	
支付的其他与投资活动有关的现金	Other cash paid relating to investing activities	33	
现金流出小计	Sub-total of cash outflows	34	
投资活动产生的现金流量净额	Net cash flows form investing activities	35	
三．筹资活动产生的现金流量	Cash Flows from Financing Activities		
吸收权益性投资所收到的现金	Proceeds from issuing shares	36	
发行债券所收到的现金	Proceeds from issuing bonds	37	
借款所收到的现金	Proceeds from borrowings	38	
收到的其他与筹资活动有关的现金	Other proceeds relating to financing activities	41	
现金流入小计	Sub-total of cash inflows	42	
偿还债务所支付的现金	Cash repayments of amounts borrowed	43	
发生筹资费用所支付的现金	Cash payments of expenses on any financing activities	44	

（续表）

项　　　目	Items	行次 NO.	金额 Amount
三．筹资活动产生的现金流量	**Cash Flows from Financing Activities**		
分配股利或利润所支付的现金	Cash payments for distribution of dividends or profits	45	
偿付利息所支付的现金	Cash payments of interest expenses	46	
融资租赁所支付的现金	Cash payments for finance leases	47	
减少注册资本所支付的现金	Cash payments for reduction of registered capital	48	
支付的其他与筹资活动有关的现金	Other cash payments relating to financing activities	51	
现金流出小计	**Sub-total of cash outflows**	52	
筹资活动产生的现金流量净额	**Net cash flows from financing activities**	53	
四．汇率变动对现金的影响	Effect of Foreign Exchange Rate Changes on Cash	54	
五．现金及现金等价物净增加额	Net Increase in Cash and Cash Equivalents	55	

现金流量表（二）

Cash Flows Statement

年度　　会外 03 表　　FORM AF-03

For the period ended　　单位：人民币 元

Monetary Unit: RMB ￥

补充资料	Supplemental Information	行次 NO.	金额 Amount
一．不涉及现金收支的投资和筹资活动	Investing and Financing Activities that do not Involve in Cash Receipts and Payments		
固定资产偿还债务	Repayment of debts by the transfer of fixed assets	56	
投资偿还债务	Repayment of debts by the transfer of investments	57	
固定资产进行投资	Investment in the form of fixed assets	58	
存货偿还债务	Repayment of debts by the transfer of investments	59	
		60/61	
二．净利润调节为经营活动的现金流量	Reconciliation of Net Profit to Cash Flows from Operating Activities		
利润	Net profit	62	
计提的坏账准备或转销的坏账	Add: Provision for bad debt or bad debt written off	63	
固定资产折旧	Depreciation of fixed assets	64	
无形资产摊销	Amortisation of intangible assets	65	
处置固定资产无形资产和其他长期资产的损失（减：收益）	Losses on disposal of fixed assets, Intangible assets and other long-term assets (less: gains)	66	
固定资产报废损失	Losses on scrapping of fixed assets	67	
财务费用	Financial expenses	68	
投资损失（减：收益）	Losses arising from investments (less: gains)	69	
递延税款贷项（减：借项）	Defered tax credit (less: debit)	70	
存货的减少（减：增加）	Decrease in inventories (less: increase)	71	
经营性应收项目的减少（减：增加）	Decrease in operating receivables (less: increase)	72	
经营性应收项目的增加（减：减少）	Increase in operating payables (less: decrease)	73	
增值税增加净额（减：减少）	Net payment on value added tax (less: net receipts)	74	
经营活动产生的现金流量净额	Net cash flows from operating activities	75	

（续表）

补充资料	Supplemental Information	行次 NO.	金额 Amount
三. 现金及现金等价物净增加情况	Net Increase in Cash and Cash Equivalents		
现金的期末余额	Cash at the end of the period	76	
减：现金的期初余额	Less: cash at the beginning of the period	77	
加：现金等价物的期末余额	Plus: cash equivalents at the end of the period	78	
减：现金等价物的期初余额	Less: cash equivalents at the beginning of the period	79	
现金及现金等价物净增加额	Net increase in cash and cash equivalents	80	

损 益 表
INCOME STATEMENT

___年度 ___季度 ___月份

For the period from _____ to _____

会外工 02 表
FORM AF1-02
单位：人民币
MONETARY UNIT: RMB ￥

项目 ITEMS	行次 LINE	本期数 CURRENT PERIOD	本年累计数 CURRENTY YEAR CUMULATIVE	上年同期累计数 LAST YEAR CUMULATIVE
产品销售收入 Sales of products				
其中：出口产品销售收入 　Including: Export sales				
减：销售折扣与折让 Less: Sales discount and allowance				
产品销售净额 Net sales of products				
减：产品销售税金 Less: Sales				
产品销售成本 　Cost of sales				
其中：出口产品销售成本 　Including: Cost of export sales				
产品销售毛利 Gross profit on sales				
减：销售费用 Less: Selling expenses				
管理费用 　General and administrative expenses				
财务费用 　Financial expenses				
其中：利息支出（减利息收入） 　Including: Interest expenses(minus interest income)				
汇兑损失（减汇兑收益） 　Exchange losses (minus exchange gains)				
产品销售利润 Profit on sales				
加：其他业务利润 Add: profit from other operations				
营业利润 Operating profit				
加：投资收益 Add: Income on investment				

（续表）

项目 ITEMS	行次 LINE	本期数 CURRENT PERIOD	本年累计数 CURRENTY YEAR CUMULATIVE	上年同期累计数 LAST YEAR CUMULATIVE
加：营业外收入 Add: Non-operating income				
减：营业外支出 Less: Non-operating expenses				
加：以前年度损益调整 Add: Adjustment of loss and gain for previous years				
利润总额 Total profit				
减：所得税 Less: Income tax				
净利润 Net profit				

附注：出口产品销售收入

  （1）外币名称和金额

    折合人民币金额

  （2）外币名称和金额

    折合人民币金额

Notes: Export sales

  (1) Foreign currency unit and amount _____

    converted into RMB

  (2) Foreign currency unit and amount _____

    converted into RMB